DAN BROWN

ALSO BY LISA ROGAK

Dogs of Courage: The Heroism and Heart of Working Dogs Around the World

The Dogs of War: The Courage, Love, and Loyalty of Military Working Dogs

And Nothing But the Truthiness: The Rise (and Further Rise) of Stephen Colbert

Michelle Obama in Her Own Words

Barack Obama in His Own Words

Haunted Heart: The Life and Times of Stephen King

A Boy Named Shel: The Life and Times of Shel Silverstein

DAN BROWN

The Unauthorized Biography

LISA ROGAK

THOMAS DUNNE BOOKS
ST. MARTIN'S GRIFFIN
NEW YORK

THOMAS DUNNE BOOKS.
An imprint of St. Martin's Press.

www.thomasdunnebooks.com
www.stmartins.com

ISBN 978-1-250-04332-0 (trade paperback)
ISBN 978-1-4668-4136-9 (e-book)

Parts of this book were previously published in the United States under the title
The Man Behind The Da Vinci Code by Andrews McMeel Publishing.

St. Martin's Griffin books may be purchased for educational, business, or promotional use. For information on bulk purchases, please contact Macmillan Corporate
and Premium Sales Department at 1-800-221-7945 extension 5442 or write special
markets@macmillan.com.

First St. Martin's Griffin Edition: May 2013

10 9 8 7 6 5 4 3 2 1

TO NEW HAMPSHIRE AND HER PEOPLE . . .
TRY AS I MIGHT, I JUST CAN'T STAY AWAY

CONTENTS

PROLOGUE

DAN BROWN SAT on a bench in the Grand Gallery of the Louvre in Paris, watching countless tourists walk by on their way to see the museum's most famous celebrity, the *Mona Lisa*. A pleasant-looking but virtually unknown American writer, he sat unnoticed by the people passing by, dressed in his usual casual style—jeans or khaki pants and a polo shirt, or perhaps a turtleneck and a slightly threadbare tweed jacket if the air was chilly. The footsteps of the hordes of pilgrims echoed off the walls of the gallery, but he was so lost in thought he didn't hear the noise.

During his numerous visits to Paris, it had become his custom to camp out in the museum for the day. The guards at the museum had grown used to seeing the American with the preppy, boy-next-door manners as he strolled through the hallways looking lost in thought. On this trip, he aimed to do just a little more research for his novel-in-progress, which would be his fourth published work of fiction. Though he and his wife, Blythe, would spend a good chunk of their time in museums and libraries in the city and interviewing experts, it was absolutely critical to get the details about the Louvre—the dimensions, how each gallery and hallway looked from a variety of different angles—just right. After all, the museum would play a featured role in the new book—along with Leonardo da Vinci, the creator of its most famous painting.

When he wasn't wandering around the Louvre, Brown liked to roam the main avenues and back alleys of Paris to puzzle out sticking points in the upcoming novel's story line or to figure out into which chapter it would be best to insert an obscure fact he had dug up from a sixteenth-century book.

But this time, as he watched the tourists walk by, Brown wasn't trying to flesh out a particular plot point or ruminate on the latest fact he had learned about Da Vinci. The truth was that he was worried beyond belief that his fourth novel would follow the same path as his previous three—*Digital Fortress, Angels & Demons,* and *Deception Point*—and that his dream of becoming a successful full-time novelist would never come true. *Everything* in his career was riding on this novel.

Though critics were enthusiastic about the stories and his writing, only a few thousand copies of each book were sold within the first few months of their publication, the brief make-or-break window when a new novel could hope to find an audience. Without a major success now, any interest in subsequent books by him, from both publishers and readers, would inevitably be lost in the crowd of the hundreds of new thrillers published each season, all vying for a scrap of the public's attention.

Dan Brown had been toiling away for months researching this fourth novel, which revolved around the little-known codes that Leonardo da Vinci had placed in his masterpieces—some as jokes, others as clues to hidden history in Christianity. Though Brown was known to his editors and agent for handing in lengthy novel outlines that included the minutest details of plot and characterization, the outline for this book was by far his most comprehensive. At over two hundred pages, it left little room for doubt or distraction. Brown knew which tricks he wanted to pull out of his hat to move the plot along and surprise the reader, and when. He was confident he could devise a cliffhanger at the end of most chapters—a real challenge when some were only a page long. In fact, brevity was turning out to be one of his trademarks.

His publisher, Doubleday, was enthusiastic enough about the book to pay him a $400,000 advance for his fourth and fifth novels, even after the disappointing performances of his first three. But Brown was familiar enough with the crapshoot of publishing to know that even pouring significant marketing muscle and money into a book didn't guarantee it would become a best-seller—or that the publisher would recoup its investment in the advance and production costs. You could lead a reader into a bookstore, but you couldn't make him buy your book. Millions of dollars could be spent in advertising and publicity. But in the end a book could still flop, especially if the author's previous novels had sold modestly, as Brown's had.

He was worried because this was probably his last chance to make it. If, despite his best efforts and Doubleday's, his fourth novel sank without a trace, his fifth novel would still be published, but it probably wouldn't receive more than the bare minimum of attention from the marketing department. And his once-promising career as a novelist would be over. He'd have no choice but to return to his previous career, teaching high school English.

Brown had developed his latest novel's story line and planned the research with all this weighing heavily on his mind. He deliberately chose a controversial topic that would be so shocking to millions of people around the world that it was bound to gain media attention. Publishers know that controversy sells books, and they pray for an outraged national figure to call for a boycott of a book. Of course, this usually backfires, sending sales through the roof and making both publishers and authors very happy.

So Dan Brown was anxious about his prospects, but he didn't dare reveal his doubts to Stephen Rubin, the publisher of Doubleday, or to Jason Kaufman, his editor, a new arrival from Simon & Schuster who had convinced Rubin to let him buy Brown's next two books, and who could lose his job or squander his own capital with colleagues with a couple of expensive flops.

Brown probably couldn't even express his anxiety to his own literary agent, Heide Lange, who—should the book flop—would face the challenge of finding another publisher for a client who had proved to be a liability to his previous publishers. Doubleday was the third major New York publishing house to publish Brown's fiction, and there weren't more than a handful of places left for him to go.

Only one person knew the true extent of his concern: Blythe, his wife and companion for more than a decade, who was his equal partner when it came to researching each book. Sure, the research trips to Europe were fun and the money was good, especially the first advance payment from Doubleday, which was then the biggest check Brown had received in his writing career. But both Blythe and Dan knew he was down to the wire with this book. It simply had to work. Or else he'd spend each day of the rest of his life with chalk dust on his hands, facing a job he'd tried to escape by pursuing a dream he hadn't achieved.

The pressure was sometimes overwhelming, and he occasionally thought that returning to teaching would be a welcome relief. In a way, he'd be doing the same work: introducing his audience to obscure facts and giving them a variety of entertaining ways to retain the information. In fact, in some ways teaching was better than writing, because it provided Brown with instant feedback about his storytelling technique. One well-placed groan or laugh from a student would confirm that he was on the right track. And seeing the lightbulb go on over a student's head when he finally got it—well, that was the best feeling in the world. As a writer, he received feedback, other than from his editors or agent, only when a reader wrote to tell him he didn't like the book, or that he was a lousy writer, or to point out an error. And that feedback usually came a year or more after he had finished writing the manuscript and had long ago moved on to a new novel.

Throughout his life, Dan Brown was not one to go after a task halfheartedly or to give up before he had proven to himself he had given it his all. He didn't give up on the songwriting career he had pursued after college until he had spent several years knocking on doors in Los Angeles, and he didn't want to quit now. He was so close he could feel it.

But in this highly competitive business, the odds were against him. After pouring his heart and soul and the better part of six years into researching and writing three novels that, while critically acclaimed, had sold around twenty-six thousand copies in all, Brown had decided that if his next two novels performed the same as his first three, he would do the same thing he did before: tie up the loose ends and either find something else to do or return to the classroom.

After all, by all rights, he shouldn't even be here. As a rule, publishers don't back relatively unknown novelists with much marketing muscle or money. And so while his publishers took care of getting his three novels into print and then into the stores, the truth is that it was primarily up to Brown to get the word out about his books.

And he did, once again working together with his wife. Blythe handled the publicity for her husband's novels—writing press releases, contacting reporters and producers, and setting up interviews—while all Dan had to do was to show up, in between researching and plotting out his next novel, of course.

Interestingly, there were two books by Dan Brown that neither wanted the general public to know about, because they feared they would deflect the spotlight from his novels. *187 Men to Avoid: A Survival Guide for the Romantically Frustrated Woman* was a mercifully short, cheeky humor book published in 1995 under the pseudonym of Danielle Brown that advised women to steer clear of men who, among other things, "think farting is cute" and "know more than 10 slang words for breasts."

The Bald Book came out in 1998, just after *Digital Fortress*, his first novel, was published. Although Blythe was listed as the author and illustrator on this tiny tome whose aim was to make bald and balding men feel better with lame jokes and simply drawn cartoons, the truth is that Dan himself wrote the book, which included such gems as "You're more streamlined" and "Faster cleanup."

Whether Brown was researching little-known art history, promoting his novels to the media, or working to distance himself from his other books, he reveled in spending every day working side by side with Blythe, which he couldn't do if he was teaching English to high school freshmen again.

And so he decided to stake his future on a little-known premise that had been whispered about for centuries in art and religious circles but was not widely known to the general public. Once it was revealed in popular form, in the pages of Brown's new novel, it was certain to generate controversy—especially within the Catholic Church.

But, again, nothing in this business was guaranteed. So still he fretted.

He watched another knot of tourists wander by for a glimpse of the Mona Lisa, and tried not to worry.

■ ■ ■

Of course, fast-forward just a few years, and the picture looked totally different. After his fourth novel, The Da Vinci Code, was published in March 2003, Brown's fortunes changed dramatically. Now, whenever he showed up at a book signing or was featured on the Today show or Good Morning America, he was greeted in the same fashion as most celebrities or rock stars: with hordes of screaming fans, lines around the block, and everyone from Charles Gibson to Matt Lauer—even Steven Tyler of Aerosmith—hanging on his every word.

Though he was plainly pleased by the adoration and clamor for his book, a slight deer-in-headlights look would fleetingly appear on his face as if to project his real worry: How could he ever write another book that would match the success of this one? Plus, he was clearly uncomfortable being the focus of everyone's attention, which was a major reason why he abandoned his musical career.

Today, Dan Brown is a mega-best-selling author, with more than eighty million copies of the novel he was fretting over—*The Da Vinci Code*—in print around the world. The book spent more than two years in one of the top five positions on the *New York Times* hardcover best-sellers list. In all, his novels have sold more than 200 million copies around the world, and have been translated into fifty-two different languages.

In the wake of becoming a bona fide celebrity—and *The Da Vinci Code* becoming a universally recognized title—Brown said that no one is more surprised at its success than he, especially after the doubt he experienced. "I worked very hard on this book, and I'm not surprised that people are enjoying it," he said, "but I really didn't expect that this many people would be enjoying it quite this much."

That's quite an understatement, but then again, his words could actually be part of a meticulously crafted campaign; media coaches and book publicists everywhere know that readers prefer their mega-selling authors to fall into the "Aw-shucks, I just wrote a book" category. Such a carefully chosen, self-effacing posture can work wonders to moderate any jealousy of his success that might eventually hurt book sales.

Needless to say, the book's success caused his life to change radically. In a matter of months, he went from living a relatively open life where he cheerfully agreed to talk to any newspaper or TV reporter who showed up at his door, to putting a moratorium on any and all media interviews. Today, out of necessity, he lives a relatively cloistered life. He jealously guards his privacy and asks his friends and business colleagues to do the same on his behalf. He holds no illusions about being able to return to the quiet life he led before *The Da Vinci Code* turned him into a celebrity in some quarters, and into persona non grata in others.

There's obviously much more to the story. The critical response to *The Da Vinci Code* was more diverse—and, at one extreme, much more venomous—than Brown or his publisher could have ever anticipated. Dan Brown and his novel became the target of ecclesiastical vituperation unrivaled by any author in the history of modern-day book publishing.

Today, he appears in public only if it involves one of the three causes close to his heart: the New Hampshire Writers' Project, a nonprofit health clinic called Families First, or Phillips Exeter Academy, the elite private boarding school that, it could be said, raised him, nurtured him, and gave him the tools necessary to foster the imagination responsible for bringing *The Da Vinci Code* to the world.

In truth, Dan Brown's desire to live a fully creative life, first by trying to make it in the music business, then by penning short humor books, and finally by writing novels full time, closely resembles the trials, tribulations, and constant cliffhangers that Robert Langdon—his alter ego and the star of *Angels & Demons*, *The Da Vinci Code*, *The Lost Symbol*, and his latest, *Inferno*—confronts in almost every chapter. Robert Langdon, a Harvard professor of religious iconology who refers to himself as a symbologist, faces countless hair-raising and often life-threatening challenges in both novels, each taking place over the course of twenty-four hours.

In other words, there were numerous occasions in Dan Brown's life when he almost didn't make it, where he was tempted to give up and return to his former, predictable—albeit safe—life.

It all began in Exeter, New Hampshire.

DAN BROWN

CHAPTER ONE

OF SECRET CODES
AND SECRET SOCIETIES

"**I GREW UP** in a household where riddles and codes were just part of the way we had fun," said Dan Brown, recalling his childhood. "On Christmas morning where most kids would find their presents under the tree, my siblings and I might find a treasure map with codes that we would follow from room to room and eventually find our presents hidden somewhere else in the house. So for me, codes have always been fun.

"I also grew up in a house of mathematics, music, and language. And codes and ciphers really are the fusion of all of those languages."

His mother and father set up the first Christmas morning treasure hunt when Dan was ten years old. Instead of waking to a pile of brightly wrapped presents, he found a poem. While he didn't disclose what the poem said, he did say the poem provided clues that led Dan and his sister, Valerie, who was only six at the time—their younger brother, Gregory, hadn't been born yet—to another room in the house. There, he spotted an index card with the letter *E* scrawled on it along with another poem.

This game continued until he had read four more poems and picked up four more index cards with the letters *C, O, P,* and *T* written on them. The poem found with the last index card instructed the siblings that the letters would spell out the name of their Christmas gift when arranged in the correct order.

It didn't take long for Dan and Valerie to figure out that

their present was a trip to Epcot Center at Disney World in Florida. The children loved solving the puzzle, and their parents enjoyed the challenge of planning and designing the treasure hunt so much that the Christmas morning treasure hunt continued as a Brown family tradition until the last child, Gregory, left home in 1993.

When asked if there had ever been a holiday when he and his brother and sister were unable to find a clue or a present, he replied, "Gee, I hope not. I have very kind parents. Eventually they would show us." But then Brown commented that the first thing he would do the next time he was at his parents' house would be to look in a closet for any presents they might have missed. Though his comment could have just been a bit of lighthearted banter with his interviewer, it could also point to Brown's natural suspicions that powerful people—in this case, one's parents—*always* keep secrets, and that it would be a great, fun challenge to discover the truth.

■ ■ ■

"I grew up surrounded by the clandestine clubs of Ivy League universities, the Masonic lodges of our Founding Fathers, and the hidden hallways of early government power," said Dan Brown. "New England has a long tradition of elite private clubs, fraternities, and secrecy."

All you need to know about what makes Dan Brown tick can be found in Exeter, New Hampshire, founded in 1638, a town on the seacoast of the Granite State, where he has spent three-quarters of his life. More specifically, you'd have to look in the halls and people of Phillips Exeter Academy, an elite college preparatory boarding school for grades nine through twelve. It has educated members of the Dupont and Getty families and produced political notables including roommates David Eisenhower and Fred Grandy—whose public visibility began on the 1970s TV show *The Love Boat*—and Arthur Schlesinger Jr. Other writers who attended the Academy include Gore Vidal, George Plimpton, Joyce Maynard, Donald Hall, and Booth Tarkington. For centuries, the culture of most New England prep schools has been characterized by a combination of noblesse oblige and elitism so that generations of students at not only Phillips Exeter but also other schools, including Deerfield, Phillips Andover, and Choate Rosemary Hall, graduate with a sense of entitlement and privilege that alone can carry them for the rest of their lives in many cases.

Given his fascination with secret societies and history, and his family's emphasis on education and love of deciphering codes and puzzles, it's not at all surprising that Dan Brown chose the subjects for his novels that he has. After all, he not only grew up in Exeter, New Hampshire, but he also was shaped by centuries of the lives of citizens who came before him.

Compare a present-day glance down Water Street—the main drag through town—with scenes of Exeter as shown on postcards from the early twentieth century, and it's clear that the architecture of the town has changed very little through the years. In fact, many of today's shopkeepers take pride in the tin ceilings and polished woodwork that hearken back to an earlier, more genteel time.

There are some who would say that the gentility and aggressive pursuit of everything intellectual bred in this refined seacoast town never left. A good part of the reason for this can be attributed to Phillips Exeter Academy, founded a century and a half after the town got its start as a British base for shipping and inland exploration.

But from its earliest days, Exeter forged a "school town" reputation. In fact, the townspeople placed such a high premium on educating their young that the first formal classes for children began in 1640, only two years after the first settlement was carved out of the thickly forested land by the Reverend John Wheelwright in 1638. The town's emphasis on intellectual pursuits never wavered through the years, and by the early 1800s the town contained a number of schools, ranging from one-room schoolhouses to well-known teaching academies in addition to Phillips Exeter, which by that time had started to admit students from other states.

Like many small towns throughout New England at the time, Exeter had various chapters of fraternal organizations, private clubs, and social groups where businessmen, immigrants, and schoolteachers could network and participate in activities they enjoyed with like-minded citizens. Some of these groups were steeped in history, while others were just informal gatherings; most were segregated by gender. In addition, many of the societies had a public face—often involved in raising money for local charities and the poor—and a private side, replete with special dress, manners of addresses, rituals, and membership initiations that were kept well hidden from the eyes of outsiders.

One of the most popular social organizations in town was the Improved Order of Red Men, a group that had descended from a group called the Sons of Liberty, which dated back to 1765, when it was founded by future Boston Tea Party participants. The national fraternal organization dictated that its members should love and respect the American flag, help others through organized charitable programs, and actively support the democratic way of life while preserving the traditions and history of the United States. Members attended meetings in full Indian costume and headdress; the female counterpart of the group was the Degree of Pocahontas. The Order was popular from Victorian times up through the 1960s; membership hit its peak at a half million in the 1930s, and today is estimated to be around 30,000 nationwide.

Another group in town was known as the Star in the East Lodge, Number 59 of the Free and Accepted Masons Orient, also known as the Freemasons. This lodge was formed in 1857, with the stipulation that meetings be conducted "on Thursday of the week of the full moon." The Freemasons are still active in Exeter and currently meet on the second floor of the Masonic Hall on Water Street.

Other "secret societies" that have been active in Exeter through the nineteenth and twentieth centuries include the Independent Order of Odd Fellows, the St. Albans Royal Arcanum, the Good Templars, and the Knights of Pythias, all groups that Dan Brown has drawn on to some extent in his novels.

An interesting side note: Dan Brown was not the first acclaimed author with the same last name to come from Exeter or to base his characters on people in the town. Alice Brown (1856-1948) was born in nearby Hampton Falls, New Hampshire, and was a renowned author of regional fiction, including the works *Tiverton Tales* and *Meadow Grass*. She also wrote nonfiction, including a study of Robert Louis Stevenson and a book of travel essays about England. Her play *Children of the Earth* won her a $10,000 prize in 1914.

Like Dan Brown, Alice Brown was a teacher. She taught school in Exeter for several years at Robinson Seminary, a renowned school for girls in the second half of the nineteenth century. Also like her latter-day counterpart, she left Exeter when she was in her twenties and headed for Boston, where she was able to write full time.

Unlike Dan Brown, however, she never returned to live permanently in New Hampshire, and later in her life, she wrote less and less as popular taste turned away from the regional fare in which she specialized. She stopped writing completely in 1935. It's unlikely that the two Browns were related.

The acclaimed author of *The World According to Garp*, John Irving, was born in Exeter and grew up on Front Street, down the block from Dan Brown's childhood home.

■ ■ ■

Phillips Exeter Academy, founded in 1781, is at once ancient—the oldest building, Nathaniel Gilman House, was built in 1735 and predates the Academy—and modern: Its student body currently hails from twenty-nine different countries, the library is state-of-the-art, and the overriding philosophy of the school is to look to the future. Though many boarding schools maintain a campus that is somewhat removed from the main town or city where it is located, Phillips Exeter is unique in that it is right in the middle of downtown Exeter, allowing students to conveniently walk to shops on Water Street or Front Street, and they consider the central community gathering place in town—the Common—to be an extension of the school.

However, like most private New England boarding schools, Phillips Exeter Academy is a world apart from the bustling everyday activity of townsfolk unassociated with the Academy. Essentially, Phillips Exeter is a secret society all its own, where new students quickly learn that the culture is steeped in an Us versus Them mentality. The students and faculty are insiders and people in the rest of the world become, by definition, outsiders. What goes on within its walls is largely unknown and unnoticed by the outsiders, and the insiders like to keep it that way.

This view is almost essential to the strong bonds and active learning that take place at most elite private schools, but the idea of private school as secret society may have been more firmly entrenched in Brown's spirit than in his fellow students for one simple reason: He spent his entire childhood at the school.

Not only was he a student at the Academy during grades nine through twelve, but he also basically grew up on the campus, since his father, Richard, joined the faculty two years before Dan was born.

Richard G. Brown arrived at the doors of Phillips Exeter Academy in the fall of 1962 as a new teacher of mathematics. He brought his new wife, the former Constance Gerhard, who had trained as a church organist and student of sacred music, with him.

Though Richard had not previously attended the Academy as a student, as was commonly the case for many of his colleagues on the faculty, he realized that Phillips Exeter would provide a free superior education to any children he and his wife would eventually have. So even though Richard began his career at the Academy as an outsider, his children were viewed as insiders from day one.

Together the newlyweds quickly settled into campus life as dorm parents, since faculty members were required to live on campus for the first few years of employment at the school.

The new Mr. and Mrs. Brown didn't mind in the least. They were eager to become fully involved in the daily life of the school and spend it with students and faculty who shared their love for intelligent conversation and academic pursuits. The Browns wanted to start a family of their own, and their first son, Daniel Gerhard, was born two years later at Exeter Hospital on June 22, 1964, weighing seven pounds and eight ounces. Valerie was born in 1968 followed by Gregory in 1975.

As it turns out, Dan Brown was not the first best-selling author in his family. Richard Brown was the co-author of a best-selling series of mathematics textbooks that became the recommended text in classrooms throughout the United States. *Advanced Mathematics: Precalculus with Discrete Mathematics and Data Analysis* is still used as a primary text in advanced mathematics coursework. At some point in his career, his work came to the attention of the National Security Agency, and though the then-secret government division actively recruited him, Richard Brown never worked there. He loved his job at the Academy, and though he was flattered by the NSA's pursuit, he decided he didn't want to leave teaching or uproot his family.

The Brown family was active on campus, and Richard and Connie encouraged their children to balance educational pursuits and physical activity every day as best they could. At home, however, the overriding activity was intellectual pursuit.

"When I was ten years old, the wondrous author Madeleine L'Engle introduced me to a world of mysticism and adventure,"

Brown said in later years. "Her classic, A Wrinkle in Time, was the first book I ever read more than once—four times, to be exact— and her mesmerizing concept of tesseracts got me thinking of our universe in a multidimensional way. I'm certain that the curiosity sparked by this one book played a substantial role in fueling my later interests. Perhaps it was just a function of the right book at the right moment, but never again has a fantasy grabbed me as powerfully as did A Wrinkle in Time. Oddly now, three decades later, I am starting to recapture some of that childhood excitement as similar themes of magic and mysticism work their way into my own books."

Since Phillips Exeter faculty were required to live on campus for several years before they could move to a house or apartment in town, Dan was immersed in the culture of the Academy from his earliest years, eating most meals in the dining room with his parents, and living in a dorm parent apartment nestled among student dorm rooms.

Dan attended the Exeter public schools until the ninth grade, when he enrolled in Phillips Exeter Academy. By the time he entered his freshman year in the fall of 1978, he had been thoroughly steeped in the culture of this exclusive, ancient college preparatory school, so he thought he had a real advantage over the new arrivals from across the United States and around the world. Dan may have been a faculty brat and his family may have lacked the money that many of his fellow students took for granted, but he knew the culture of Phillips Exeter inside out.

"It was a really great place to be, because there were people there from all over the world," said Susan Ordway, who attended the school and was a member of Dan's 1982 graduating class of 250 students.

By the time Dan became a freshman his parents were living off-campus, so he attended classes as a day student. He soon developed a reputation as "an outgoing kind of goofball," as Ordway described the teenage Dan Brown. "He was very fun to be with. He was quick with a joke and to point out funny things about other people, and didn't take anything too seriously, which is why I liked spending time with him," she said.

While boarding students live, eat, and sleep with other boarders and faculty and typically have little exposure with people outside of the school, the day students at private schools lead lives that resembled those of students in public school. They go home to family at the end of each day of classes and extracurricular activities. The fact that Dan became a day student after growing up on the campus meant he had a foot in both worlds. He was going to school in the insider community while living among the outsiders.

He was active in musical activities at the school, and he told his fellow students and teachers that he planned to move to Los Angeles and become a singer and songwriter after graduating from college. "He had a pretty good voice," Ordway recalled.

Though news reports of private New England schools throughout the years have been rife with stories about secret fraternities and rituals, according to Ordway, the cult role-playing game Dungeons and Dragons was about as underground as things got at Phillips Exeter, and Dan wasn't involved. "At the time, Dungeons and Dragons appealed to the social misfits on campus, and Dan was not a misfit or loner by any means," she said.

The daily schedule at the school precluded much free time for the students to get into trouble, with classes all day, then sports, which were required, followed by homework. Boarding students had to be in the dorms by nine or ten at night, and by that time Dan had been home for hours.

Pranks were a big part of blowing off steam on campus, but they tended to be the harmless variety. Most were conducted in the library, designed by the renowned Philadelphia architect Louis Kahn, because the building had a huge atrium that lent itself to stunts like throwing string across the open space above the main floor to create a spider web or dumping a slew of ping-pong balls over the edge.

Seniors were granted more freedom as graduation approached, and would often hold contests to see how many of the "major eight" rules they could break; the major eight were the eight rules that could cause a student to be expelled from Phillips Exeter, and they included everything from drinking and doing drugs, cheating, and plagiarism, to being on the roof of any building on campus.

Besides being active both physically and intellectually, at Phillips Exeter "they take pride in the fact that, if you can do nothing else, you learn to write," said Brown.

As a newly minted freshman, Dan Brown arrived in Jack Heath's English class. A mythical figure on campus, Heath had a reputation as a man of few words. Dan was thrilled he finally had a teacher who could appreciate what the fourteen-year-old Dan modestly thought of as his genius for the written word.

For his first assignment, Dan chose to write an essay about the Grand Canyon. "I described with inexhaustible prolixity the subtle hues and fissures of the limestone," he said. "Mr. Heath returned the essay doused in red pen. He had deleted 90 percent of my adjectives and given me a C-minus. At the top of the page were three words: *Simpler is better*."

When the semester was over, Dan had worked his way up to a C-plus average. As the students filed out on the last day of class, the chastened freshman faculty brat asked the teacher for some words of wisdom.

"Simpler is better," repeated the teacher.

In Dan's senior year at the Academy, Heath popped up again in his life as his baseball coach. Compared to those of other coaches at Phillips Exeter and competing teams, the signals that Heath sent to the young athletes were direct and uncomplicated. Instead of an intricate series of hand motions and head twitches to conceal the signals he wanted to send to players, Heath merely nodded toward second base if he wanted the first-base runner to attempt a steal.

At one point, Dan asked the teacher why his technique was so different from the other coaches'. As before, Mr. Heath replied, "Simpler is better."

Later on, after the success of *The Da Vinci Code*, Dan would often tell interviewers and aspiring writers the key to the success of his storytelling was the liberal use of the delete key on his computer. Though it took some time, the lessons he learned in high school finally sank in. In fact, Brown directly cited Heath's influence in helping him to pare down the novel that became *Digital Fortress*, saying he finally learned to cut back on his use of adjectives in his writing.

Interestingly, there were at least two other significant future novelists on campus when Dan was a senior at Phillips Exeter: Brooks Hansen, author of *The Chess Garden*, and Chang-Rae Lee, author of the highly acclaimed *A Gesture Life*, were members of the class of 1983, a year behind Brown. In addition, Henry Blodgett, a Wall Street analyst who was a golden boy during the tech stock boom in the late 1990s, was also a student at Phillips Exeter when Dan was there.

■ ■ ■

Another lesson Dan Brown took to heart from Phillips Exeter—and which later became evident in the numerous disciplines he incorporated into his novels—was that the best thing to aim for in life was to become a Renaissance man. After all, one of the unspoken aims of many a private school is to create students who are well-rounded, which is generally accomplished by introducing each student to as many different disciplines and topics as possible across the sciences, arts, literature, and sports. Of course, the idea is to expose students to multiple subjects before college, where they'd eventually settle down and focus on one area.

Perhaps Dan took this to heart more than other students simply because he was immersed in this philosophy from a very early age, and because he witnessed it for his entire childhood. Essentially, he was in his element when he was learning about something he knew absolutely nothing about.

This curiosity about everything and the desire to learn would continue after high school. He tried his hand at the music business as a singer-songwriter after college, but he quickly learned he didn't have the stomach for such an intense and cutthroat business, and he discovered he didn't like to perform in front of people. However, more important, music didn't provide him with the opportunity to incorporate a number of different subjects into one livelihood—or to learn about something he didn't already know. That's why he loved teaching later on, because even when he was leading a classroom in a single subject like English, Brown had ample opportunity to introduce other subjects and ideas into a lesson. Throughout his life so far, it's been extremely difficult for him to focus on one discipline at a time, which is obvious in the diverse subject matter of his books.

One of the reasons he's so comfortable dealing with multiple disciplines is that two subjects the rest of the world might view as polar opposites—science and religion—coexisted peacefully and, in fact, even thrived in the Brown household. His father made his living by teaching and writing about math while his mother studied sacred music and played the organ, and they meshed seamlessly; neither one was more or less important than the other. Dan Brown was raised as a Christian and he sang in the church choir, attended Sunday school, and spent summers at church camp.

He would later reveal how his childhood had shaped him.

"Since I grew up the son of a mathematician and a church organist, I was lost from day one," he said. "Where science offered exciting proofs of its claims, whether it was photos, equations, or visible evidence, religion was a lot more demanding, constantly wanting me to accept everything on faith. Faith takes a fair amount of effort, especially for young children and especially in an imperfect world. So as a boy, I gravitated toward the solid foundations of science. But the further I progressed into this solid world of science, the mushier the ground started to get."

Dan's father was also an avid singer. One year, while Dan was a student at Phillips Exeter, he dragged a bunch of classmates to see his father play the leading role in *The Pirates of Penzance*, a production put on by a local theater group. Creativity was strongly encouraged in his family, never discouraged. "I've always known I would have to do something creative with my life," he said.

Susan Ordway remembers that Brown wanted to pursue music after high school, and that he had kept his fellow alumni updated on his pursuits, but she and her other classmates were surprised when he published his first novel, *Digital Fortress*. Surprisingly, Brown never revealed his fascination with secret societies of all stripes to other students.

"He never said or did anything in high school to indicate that he was into secret societies," said Ordway. "He had a very open and sunny personality, hung out with his buddies, and basically got along with everyone. He was just a normal, happy guy with a stable home life whose dad worked on campus. We didn't see any roots of the secret society thing in high school."

CHAPTER TWO

LEAVING THE NEST

"**WHEN I GRADUATED** from college, I had two loves: writing fiction and writing music."

After graduating from Phillips Exeter Academy in the spring of 1982, Dan Brown spent the summer traveling through Spain. That trip whetted his appetite to see more of the world; when he enrolled at Amherst College that fall he joined the school Glee Club and signed on for a world tour the following year. Brown cites the world tour as one of the best experiences he had in college, mentioning the exposure to new cultures and peoples as the most important part of the trip. "We went to thirteen or fourteen countries for a few months," he said, "and I never would have seen them otherwise. It was amazing."

While at Amherst, he played on the varsity squash team, where he later admitted losing countless matches and getting "pummeled" in national competitions. He also continued to develop his Renaissance-man side by signing up for a double major in English and Spanish.

Another formative college experience he cites was taking a class taught by Alan Lelchuk, a literary novelist who was a visiting professor of English at Amherst for several years. "He was very intense, and I just wrote and wrote," he said. Like the other students in his class, he was thrilled to have a teacher who was also working as an active, published author. At the time, however, Brown didn't view Lelchuk as a role model for his own future endeavors. The older man was simply a teacher, one who continually challenged him to do his best, much as Jack Heath had done at Phillips Exeter.

Indeed, while Brown said that Lelchuk showed him how to refine his expertise in English composition and sparked his creativity, he didn't consider a future career as a novelist while in college. Even though Brown spent most of his free time there working on a variety of creative writing projects, he said he never imagined he'd ever find a need for writing the kind of prose that Professor Lelchuk taught. Instead, he planned to apply the lessons he learned and the discipline of writing daily to the songwriting and music career he had already decided to pursue after graduation. Later on, however, he would attribute his experience in his writing class with Lelchuk with giving him the confidence to attempt his first novel a decade later.

Brown would later cite one more crucial incident that played an influential role in the years to come. It occurred during his junior year at Amherst College, when he spent a year abroad in Spain studying at the University of Seville.

As was his custom, during the year he spent in Spain, Dan decided to tackle a subject he knew little about: art history. There, the initial seed for what turned into *The Da Vinci Code* was planted by one of his professors. One day in class, the teacher gave a talk on the art of Leonardo da Vinci, complete with slide show. The professor began pointing out anomalies, hidden messages, and jokes that Da Vinci had placed in his paintings, sculptures, and drawings.

He began by showing a slide of *The Last Supper* and then casually remarking to a class full of students who were half asleep that the figure sitting to the right of Jesus in the painting was not John, as had been commonly handed down through the ages. Rather, it was a woman, and more specifically, Mary Magdalene. The professor then continued to point out other secrets in the painting, including the fact that there was no cup of wine anywhere in the picture.

This routine lecture about Da Vinci's paintings was a cata-lyst for Dan Brown's imagination. To the still-impressionable col-lege student who had a keen lifelong interest in discovering groundbreaking secrets, breaking codes, and solving puzzles, that one brief lecture sent him down a path that would eventually change his life in ways he could never have fathomed at the time.

"To art historians out there, this will not seem like news, but to most of us, the idea that a painting as famous as the *Mona Lisa* or *The Last Supper* has hidden meaning is intriguing," he said. "And when I was studying art history at the University of Seville, that was really the first time that I saw *The Last Supper* for what it truly is, which is a fresco full of codes. When you look at the *Mona Lisa* and wonder why she's smiling, you've just scratched the surface. And paintings like *Madonna of the Rocks* and *Adoration of the Magi* are just packed with hidden symbolic meaning."

In any case, Dan's eyes were opened, not only to the secret messages that Leonardo da Vinci was trying to send to viewers across the centuries, but also to a great abundance of intention-ally placed codes and messages that could occur across several works in an artist's oeuvre.

The professor had given him the gift of a brand-new pair of eyes with which he could view art in all its forms—not only visual art, but also music, literature, and religion. By the time he wrapped up his year in Spain and prepared to return to Amherst, Dan Brown believed he had learned the most important lesson of his lifetime so far. He just wasn't exactly sure what to do with it, so he filed it away for the future.

■ ■ ■

After graduating from Amherst, Brown entered into an apprenticeship of sorts with himself. Though his ultimate goal was to move to Los Angeles and make his mark on the music industry as a singer and songwriter, he felt that he needed to learn more about composing and arranging music and behind-the-scenes production work first. Plus, he needed a break after spending eight sometimes-grueling years at two of the country's most elite private schools. He suspected that his educational background wouldn't do much for him in Hollywood, and indeed, once he arrived on the West Coast, Brown discovered how much of a liability it was.

But for now, fresh out of college, he decided to bide his time in Exeter, save some money for his move, and immerse himself in making music. He bought a synthesizer and some secondhand recording equipment and began to teach himself everything he could about the technology and how he could use it to compose his own music.

One day, he was experimenting with his synthesizer and realized that a certain noise he created sounded exactly like the croak of a frog. He then composed a short musical piece in which he attempted to duplicate the sound of a frog-filled pond. He named this tune "Happy Frogs" and then proceeded to see what other animal sounds he could create on the synthesizer. He composed several other brief animal-sound songs and titled them "Suzuki Elephants," "Swans in the Mist," and "Rats." He decided to create an entire children's album—or, more accurately, a cassette—of synthesized animal songs, and soon he had completed *SynthAnimals*.

A couple of area stores around Exeter stocked the tape and a few local newspapers profiled the cassette, but *SynthAnimals* sold only a few hundred copies. Brown, however, considered it an education and a successful first effort in producing and distributing his own work. What was next? He had produced an album for kids, so now he wanted to learn how to do the same for an adult market.

He left *SynthAnimals* on the sidelines while he formed his own vanity record company called Dalliance, and in 1990 he released *Perspective*, his first full-length album aimed at adults. This time, instead of doing it all himself and making it 100 percent synthesized, Brown brought in a few friends from Phillips Exeter on the project, including Chip Beckett, who sang and played keyboards, and Earl Bethel, who played bass and guitar.

From the beginning Brown knew that he wanted his songs for adults to stand out, just as *SynthAnimals* was different from the other synthesized music being made at the time. He characterized his music in the category of top-forty, but different. "People ask, 'Who do you sound like?' and we say 'Nobody.' It's a softer kind of pop, and the lyrics are important," he said. "We try to tell a story."

As he did with *SynthAnimals*, Brown sold a few hundred copies locally, but more important, he knew he could use the album as a demo of his music to present to producers and agents in Hollywood. He had two albums for different markets under his belt, and had saved up enough money, and so in the spring of 1991 he moved to Los Angeles. He found an apartment at the Franklin Regency in Hollywood within spitting distance of the major industry players.

Although he thought his music and lyrics were good, he knew they needed some tinkering, but more important, he knew he needed to start networking and meeting people in the industry who could jump-start his music career.

He also needed to support himself while plunging into the music business, and he couldn't picture waiting tables or working in a retail store in order to make ends meet. So he got a job at Beverly Hills Preparatory School as a Spanish teacher. He viewed this as a wise networking move, since he knew that some of his students had parents in influential positions who could potentially help him leapfrog over the thousands of other wannabe singers and songwriters.

This turned out to be a good move, if only because it taught him how to interact with celebrities without getting flustered. "Parent-teacher conferences at a place like Beverly Hills Prep can get pretty interesting," he later said. "Try looking Rupert Murdoch or Michael Eisner in the eye and saying, 'Hey, your kid's a lazy bum and if he doesn't shape up, he's going to fail my course.' Now that's exciting!"

At this stage in his life he started a pattern that would last for years, in which he would essentially juggle two full-time jobs at once: a teaching job during the day and an unpaid creative job that consumed his nights and weekends. The good thing about teaching was that it gave him an entire summer to work on his music.

As he settled in to his new apartment and teaching gig, Brown got to work. He saw an ad for a business called the Creative Musicians Coalition, which distributed albums for independent artists through a nationwide catalog. He sent a copy of *SynthAnimals* to test the waters, and CMC owner Ron Wallace determined that it was good—and unique—enough to pick up for his catalog. Later, Brown would add a small spiral-bound booklet called *SynthAnimals: The Itsy-Bitsy Book of Animal Poems* that he packaged with the tape.

Once *SynthAnimals* was distributed—which proved to Brown that he had an instinct for knowing what would sell in the business—he focused his attention once again on meeting the people who could make things happen for him.

After all, among the lessons he had learned from Phillips Exeter and Amherst was one he thought would carry him far in Los Angeles: Just get your foot in the door with an influential group of people and stake your claim as a bona fide member. Then, the natural protective cliquishness inherent to most groups—especially in secret societies, and what was the music business if not a secret society?—will kick in and you'll really start to go places.

So he joined the National Academy of Songwriters, a group that seemed to fit the bill since it claimed many famous musicians as members, including Billy Joel and Prince. The organization offered aspiring songwriters moral support and instruction in both technique and navigating the business. Brown began to attend classes and workshops, and because this was the first group he had encountered since moving to California where he felt comfortable, he began hanging out at the Academy when he wasn't working or dropping off demos to agents and producers. He became friendly with a few students as well as with some staff members. One day, he struck up a conversation with Blythe Newlon, the director of artistic development for the organization.

As part of her job, Blythe showed him the ropes, gave him a few pointers, and translated the often-insular politics of the business. She also helped Brown learn the technical aspects of the craft and hone the style of his music, which tended toward soft rock.

She must have seen something in him, because shortly after they met, Blythe took Dan on as a client and decided to manage his songwriting career—arranging bookings and gigs and setting up auditions and meetings with record industry executives. This was an unusual move for Newlon; she rarely assumed a manager-client relationship with any of the songwriters at the Academy, since it fell outside the realm of her daily responsibilities at the office. In addition, it was frowned upon by her colleagues at work.

But it quickly paid off for Brown. Blythe set up meetings with influential agents and producers, and booked him in the Academy's talent showcase called the Acoustic Underground. The showcase was first presented at a club in Santa Monica called At My Place before moving to the Troubadour in West Hollywood. It was customary for singers and songwriters to audition either in person or via tape for a chance to appear in the showcase, but since Blythe was his manager, Brown never had to audition. While many of the other showcase performers tended toward the acoustic folk-music genre, Brown stood out since his music had more of a soft-rock flavor with complex instrumentation.

Paul Zollo, author of the books *Songwriters on Songwriting* and *Conversations with Tom Petty*, served as editor of *SongTalk*, the magazine the National Academy of Songwriters published for its membership, at the same time Blythe worked at the organization. He also worked with her to produce the Acoustic Underground, where he served as host.

Zollo worked in the office next to Blythe's and he and other coworkers were used to seeing Brown come by on a regular basis to talk business with her.

When the first edition of *Songwriters on Songwriting*—a compilation of interviews that were originally published in *SongTalk*—came out in 1991, Zollo received a lot of press. While others around the Academy offices noticed and offered their congratulations, one person in particular paid special attention to the media accolades that were pouring in for Zollo's book.

"I remember that Dan was extremely interested," said Zollo. "He really perked up when I came in to announce all the press I was getting." Brown's curiosity was actually quite prophetic, since it shows that even then, he knew that garnering the attention of the press—and lots of it—would be the key to success in the music business. The only problem was that he thought the media would focus on the music he created, not him personally or his performances.

It would be a hard lesson to learn, and one that would eventually send him back to New Hampshire. But before that happened, he had to see how far he could go in the music business.

It didn't take long for Brown to get his first big break, and Blythe was instrumental in making it happen: He was presented with the opportunity to release *Dan Brown*, a debut CD of his own songs on his own label—DGB Music—and he'd be backed by some of Hollywood's most talented studio musicians.

"Upon hearing Dan's work, the National Academy of Songwriters decided to adopt a hands-on approach to his career," wrote Blythe in an announcement to the trade. "We recommended he not shop for the usual record deal, but paired him instead with one of the most respected producers in pop music today."

It was an unusual arrangement for the National Academy of Songwriters to become involved in. Generally, a record label signs a contract with an artist and then pays for everything connected with producing, distributing, and promoting an album. Once the album is released, all revenue derived from the sale goes directly to the label, and it could be months or years before an artist sees a penny from the sales. Indeed, some never make any money.

"Brown used his rough demos and some fancy footwork to convince British Record Producer of the Year Barry Fasman to help him make a record," she continued. "Barry agreed to produce an album based on the quality of Dan's songwriting and vocal ability. . . . We fully expect Dan Brown will someday be included in the ranks of our most successful members, talents like Billy Joel, Paul Simon, and Prince."

The industry perked up at news of Brown's debut once Barry Fasman came onboard as producer; his résumé reads like a *Who's Who* of the music industry. He has produced and/or arranged albums for Johnny Mathis, Diana Ross, Barry Manilow, Billy Joel, and Air Supply, among others, and he composed and arranged scores for numerous movies, including *JFK, My Mom's a Werewolf,* and *Hellgate.* He won the award for British Record Producer of the Year in 1982.

The studio musicians were no slouches either. They included Madonna's bassist, the drummer for the Doobie Brothers, and a saxophonist who had played with Michael Jackson and Paul McCartney. So the stakes were huge, and optimism about Dan Brown and his future as a singer and songwriter was considerable.

With this stellar backing from industry veterans, Brown felt confident to invest in his future. And so, because the burden of financing the production and first pressing of the CD fell squarely on his shoulders, he went into overdrive. He begged and borrowed money from everyone he had ever known, maxed out his credit cards, and worked overtime tutoring students to come up with the money that would allow him to make a self-titled debut CD.

The money required to foot the bill of the studio production employed for *Dan Brown* was substantial. After all, a band of professional musicians had to be paid for their time, and studio and mastering time had to be reserved. And of course, there was Barry Fasman's fee that had to be covered.

"I always wondered where the bucks came from," said Ron Wallace of Creative Musicians Coalition. "I also wondered why the Academy would back him and how they'd benefit, especially since they represented so many other people. Why would they put their money into him? I guessed that maybe somewhere, sometime, there was a sugar daddy involved."

■ ■ ■

Unlike others who moved to Los Angeles dreaming of success in the entertainment industry and discovering that rejection is the name of the game, Brown was not bothered by competition or the seemingly constant rejection.

He discovered that he possessed a fortitude that was extremely rare among other aspiring young artists. Essentially, Brown couldn't understand how others just like him could fall into a deep depression and give up after only a few months of receiving countless rejection letters. He thought he was missing something because he viewed each rejection as instruction in how he could try harder. With that realization, he knew that Phillips Exeter was responsible.

"Exeter vaccinated me against the fear of failure," he said. "The world didn't stop when an English essay was returned with the word *INCINERATE* stamped in bright red letters across the top."

But he soon learned his connection to Phillips Exeter could be a curse as well.

"Most of what Exeter taught me wouldn't qualify as particularly relevant to real life," he said after he had spent about a year in Hollywood, detailing the countless missteps and outright howlers he had committed. For one, in the beginning, he regularly wore a coat and tie to meetings with agents and producers. "Not even lawyers wear coats and ties in Hollywood," he wryly observed.

He would also casually let it slip that he was educated at Phillips Exeter and Amherst College, a definite blunder in an industry filled with self-made millionaires who just happened to be high school dropouts. Indeed, he quickly discovered that his background had turned into more of a liability than an advantage. "In a field glorifying long hair, tattoos, and waking up drunk in the gutter, a firm grasp of the English language is not exactly a prerequisite for success," he noted.

In addition, he saw that he shared little in common with his fellow aspiring songwriters: Not only did they not come from privileged educational backgrounds, but they were also willing to do things that Brown—with his native Yankee values and good-guy personality—weren't. This included endless socializing and schmoozing, which of course led to abuse of alcohol and drugs. He even saw several of his West Hollywood neighbors turn to prostituting themselves or resorting to the casting couches of the music industry, all for a shot at the big time.

Spending his days in the classroom seemed to underscore those differences. "I find that teaching a great class is as rewarding as writing a great song," he said. "Also, with all the Hollywood hype, classrooms have an uncanny way of keeping you grounded in reality. Regardless of what happens with music, I'll continue teaching forever. Everything I've accomplished in my life I owe to my education."

Well, almost. He owed a lot to Blythe, too, and he knew it. By the time production had begun on his debut CD, the two had become lovers, though no one around them was aware of the change in the dynamic of their relationship, since they chose to keep it well hidden.

They must have done a good job. "I remember we were all surprised when we found out they were romantically entwined," said Zollo.

It made sense that Blythe and Dan decided to keep their relationship a secret from other people, at least initially. For one, she was taking charge of his musical career, and as is the case today, it could have easily been misinterpreted as a power-tripping female boss exerting control over her younger client, a scenario that could have been rife for later accusations of sexual harassment should things go sour.

However, probably the larger issue for the couple was that she was twelve years his senior, and although they were living in Los Angeles, where presumably anything goes, back in the early 1990s the idea of an older woman getting into a serious relationship with a younger man might have raised eyebrows.

"People always assume it's all about the sex," said Susan Winter, coauthor of the book *Older Women, Younger Men*. "This woman obviously saw this man's potential creativity and passion deep within him, and she couldn't stand to not have that emerge. It's like a diamond beneath a pile of dirt. To women like her, older men don't present a challenge."

Blythe could have picked any one young man from the thousands who passed through the door of the Academy every year. But she picked Dan. Like Ron Wallace of CMC, she undoubtedly saw his talent and started the wheels turning by providing him with the resources necessary to give it a shot. In essence, she was a catalyst for his creativity, and she believed in him so strongly that she was willing to step outside of her safe role at the Academy and risk raising the ire of her coworkers.

At the same time, Brown gained from the relationship as well. "Men inherently need to feel appreciated and see their dreams realized," said Winter. "Imagine that the person who sees your greater potential and supports your vision also has the means to help you get there. That's pretty powerful."

Besides sharing a love of music, Dan and Blythe soon realized that they both had a keen interest in art history, specifically in the work of Leonardo da Vinci. When Dan heard this, he told

Blythe about the art history class he had taken at the University of Seville and what the professor had said about the secret codes that appear throughout his paintings and drawings. Blythe nodded. She was quite familiar with the theory through her own study of the artist and his works. Indeed, in later years, Brown would refer to her as "a Da Vinci fanatic."

And though Brown has frequently referred to his now-wife as an art historian in media interviews, it appears as though her interest in all things Da Vinci is an avocation, not a primary vocation. She developed her passion through her own study— not in the academic world. "I've heard Dan refer to Blythe as an art historian, a specialty she must have acquired since leaving the Academy, as she wasn't an art historian then," said Zollo.

In any case, their shared passion in Da Vinci helped them connect with each other, as an intimate knowledge of art history wasn't something that was readily found among denizens of the music industry. And so, Dan and Blythe began to spend time together outside of the Academy. To Newlon, who had spent years in the shark-infested waters of the Hollywood music industry, Brown was a breath of fresh air. For one, he was a nice guy. There was also an authenticity to him, with a touch of naïveté that quickly endeared him to her.

■ ■ ■

Once the CD *Dan Brown* was released, Blythe pulled out all the stops to get Brown noticed. She prepared press releases and arranged for Dan to talk with reporters and editors, but her major goal was to get attention in the industry in the form of gigs, articles in the trade press, and an agent. In one of her letters to the trade, she wrote, "The album is one of the most impressive independent projects we here at NAS have heard. Judging from the album he's put together, we think he'll make somebody a pile of money in the process.

"We believe Dan Brown is an artist destined to become a major talent. The original pressing of his debut album could very well become a collector's item."

Well, yes. But not for the reasons she envisioned back then. But in any case, as evidenced by his songs, voice, music, and appearance, Brown was being molded and promoted as a brainy but sensitive young singer who had a bit of the tortured soul about him. On the back of the CD insert is this famous snippet from a Robert Frost poem: "Two roads diverged in a wood, and I—I took the one less traveled by, And that has made all the difference." The adjacent photo shows him walking away from the camera on a snowy day.

Another promotional photo shows him wearing glasses and a vintage admiral's jacket while he holds onto one end of a chain connected to a graffiti-covered wooden fence. He's leaning away from the fence and looking pensively at the ground.

Through most of the album, Brown's voice and style resemble that of Shaun Cassidy and Rex Smith, pop singers popular with teenage girls in the 1970s, with the occasional hint of Barry Manilow. The instrumentation and arrangements are lush and just as professional as any early 1990s soft rock release. With elements of smooth jazz and occasional saxophone riffs reminiscent of Kenny G, the music on *Dan Brown* would fit right into the playlist of any adult contemporary radio station.

In several of the songs, it almost seems like Brown was trying on a variety of personas so that both he and his production team could see which one was most likely to fly with his audience. "If You Believe in Love" is a catchy tune in the form of a heartfelt ballad filled with romantic visions along with a liberal dose of piano riffs:

> *Don't let yourself be lonely*
> *Don't lock yourself away.*

By contrast, "976-LOVE" would appear to be a serious mis-step, since the quiet, brainy image that was presented in the photos of Dan on the CD seems at odds with lyrics that serve as a pulsing paean to phone sex.

> *For a two-dollar minute*
> *I can make you mine.*

Foreshadowing the themes of his future novels, the album is also filled with religious imagery. "Real" is a devotional to his one true love, where he speaks of his eternal commitment:

> *I forsake these vows that bind me*
> *I renounce this silent faith.*

"Hey Baby It's You" picks up the beat. In this bouncy pop tune, Dan tells the object of his desire that he's in love with her, and will be with her forever.

In fact, the vast majority of the songs on the album make it sound like he's pledging his undying love to Blythe.

The musical arrangement in "Shed My Skin" contains traces of a heartfelt lighters-in-the-air arena ballad, while in the lyrics Brown tells his sweetheart that this is the first time he's been in love and that the women he's known in the past have never really known the man behind the mask. Then, in "Not a Day Goes By," Brown sings about a love lost, where he hid his true feelings from the woman of his dreams.

As for the song "Angel of Love," it almost sounds as if a virgin has offered herself up to the singer for one night, and then decided to stay because she realizes she has found her one true love. Brown sings:

> *I'm trading my wings*
> *For a lover instead*

And try as he might, it seems like Brown just couldn't keep his educational background under wraps. In "Sweet Pleasure of Pain," the last song on the album, a couple of terms that Brown uses seem to come straight from a textbook about some unnamed foreign country. The very first line in the song is:

When the earth is a Kuhlstihl berth.

Huh? And then this:

*You're feeling like the shore
In a Kampuchea war.*

(For the uninitiated, Kampuchea was another term for the Cambodian Communist party more often known as the Khmer Rouge.)

Throughout the album, there's not much depth to Brown's voice, which is breathy and frequently overdubbed, with very little vibrato and not a lot of range. Also, the background instrumentals often feature contrapuntal lines and melodies that tend to overpower his thin voice. While not terribly complex, the songs do fit the pop formula of the time.

"May I Have This Dance" is a sugary-sweet ballad in which the singer invites the potential love of his life to come with him because "life they call a tango." After admitting that he essentially spent his life alone before he met this woman, the singer then tells her that he's decided to throw caution to the wind and risk it all for her love.

But the most fascinating song on the eponymous CD by far is the first track, "Birth of a King," since both the title and the lyrics could easily be interpreted as a brief outline for the story of the Holy Grail that Brown would later successfully employ in *The Da Vinci Code*. In the song, a lone man has traveled far and wide to find the woman of his dreams, who has been trapped in a castle for years. When the man finally arrives, he rescues her from her sad, solitary existence.

The second verse in "Birth of a King" echoes some of the chase scenes Brown later wrote in his Robert Langdon novels:

> *You race alone*
> *Down twisting marble stairways*

In the end, *Dan Brown* the CD didn't come close to fulfilling the dreams that Dan Brown had for it for one reason and one reason alone: He felt uncomfortable in the spotlight. This may have had its roots in his New Hampshire upbringing, where the message handed down by generations of old stoic Yankees was that you don't brag about your accomplishments.

"He could have been a Barry Manilow if he wanted to," said Ron Wallace. "Barry started out very klutzy, but the essence and musical talent was there, and he had to be trained by the industry to make him who he was." Wallace remembered that in some of Brown's early interviews, he said that he didn't want to be in the public eye and perform for people, but he liked creating the music. The problem was that his music was pop, and it put him in a position where he *had* to be a Barry Manilow in order for his music to be heard.

"I just don't think Dan wanted to dance in front of the public," said Wallace. "Songwriting was good for him because he didn't have to perform, but once he had to show who he is, he didn't want that. He had the talent, but he didn't want to get out there onstage and dance because he knew he'd trip over his own feet. And he told me that he just didn't feel comfortable being onstage."

Was he really a good singer? "When you're used to getting countless tapes in all day long with music that isn't well done, maybe a synthesizer with a drum machine thrown in, music that is well thought out and professional really stands out," said Wallace. "Dan was really good; he could really sing and the instrumentals were creative. I could tell this guy was serious about what he was doing."

But to become a successful singer, either in 1993 when Brown was working at it or today, it's almost impossible to do it by staying in the recording studio. A singer has to perform. Wallace remembered that after his debut album came out, Brown was concerned that few copies had sold. "But that's the way it is, especially for a self-titled debut CD," said Wallace. "The only purpose for that is to promote the artist, not to sell to the general public. Most artists just don't get that. To make it in the music business, you've got to be a performer."

Brown countered with the opinion that his image was at odds with the norm for the business and the time. Yet, it was clear that he resented having his image overhauled and molded into a genre that would easily fit into a categorized bin in a record store.

"Do I really look like someone cut out for MTV?" he asked. "I don't think so. I belong in a classroom; the world isn't ready for a pale, balding geek shaking his booty on national TV—not a pretty picture."

It's always been difficult to move up from the level of aspiring musician sending out demo tapes and trying to crash industry parties to the next, where heavy hitters in the business will pay attention, at least for a few minutes. When Brown was trying to do just that in the early 1990s, the Internet didn't exist on a widespread scale. Today, an independent artist with a dynamic Web site and a little bit of moxie has the potential to develop a following, but even today, a singer needs to perform to get past a certain level.

"If you pick up a CD, you're going to hear the music, not the artist," said Ron Wallace. "If you've seen that artist in performance once and you like him, it's a whole different experience. And now you're buying the CD because you like the artist, not because you necessarily heard and liked the music. You're going to sell more CDs in one night at a performance than you will in one year paying $10,000 for an ad in a magazine."

Besides being told that he had to perform in order to get anywhere, Brown also resented having people who were not as educated or as intelligent as he was telling him they knew what was best for his music and career and how he had to look and act. But Wallace said this is the nature of the business.

"If he would have given himself up to the industry, he would have easily become a household name," he added.

■ ■ ■

But even before *Dan Brown* was released, Brown was already thinking of ditching Hollywood and moving back to New Hampshire. And he was elated when Blythe said she would come with him. One report said he'd fallen hard for someone in the business and they were planning to elope. In describing his attraction to the as-yet-unnamed Blythe Newlon, Brown said, "She's smart, funny, creative, beautiful, and best of all, she doesn't let me get away with anything." He added that she would paint and cook while he would write, record, and teach.

"We're planning to trade in the BMW and Mercedes for a couple of used mountain bikes and get back to reality," he said. "I can't wait. I'm really ready for a change."

In addition to a three-thousand-mile move, he was making plans to switch to his other great love during his college years: writing. However, at the same time, he still toiled away on a follow-up album to *Dan Brown.*

As would become his habit with his writing career later on, Brown was already well into work on a new project even before his old one was released. He had no guarantees, but he worked away at his new CD with the full assumption that it would be produced and released successfully. In referring to *Angels & Demons*, the CD he would release in 1995, all he would say was, "I'm writing a new record right now, a lot of inner turmoil stuff, you know, the usual." He would complete work on the CD after he and Blythe moved to New Hampshire, and indeed, this album would reveal his disillusionment with the music business.

But for now, while he was still in California, he knew he had to play the Hollywood game and put a positive face on everything. After all, despite his self-professed fish-out-of-water status in Hollywood, he nevertheless had learned how to speak the language of his cohorts by exaggerating and taking liberties with the facts whenever possible, or at least spinning them with his own unique interpretation. He would discover later that this talent transferred quite well to writing fiction, and in fact, his propensity for stretching the facts while steadfastly maintaining he spoke nothing but the truth would later provide significant fuel for his most rabid critics.

So in June 1993, he suddenly announced to friends and colleagues that he was moving back to New Hampshire, and Blythe was coming with him. He further surprised everyone with the news that he had secured a publishing deal in New York, and he was planning to move east for only a year or so to allow him to write. In typical Hollywood parlance, he neglected to mention that his "deal" was for a goofy little humor book entitled *187 Men to Avoid*. As was the case with *SynthAnimals*, Brown considered his first book a way to learn about a new industry and perhaps get his foot in the door of a trade that had real potential.

Before they moved east, however, Dan and Blythe decided to splurge on one last vacation. During the second week of April 1993, the couple flew to Tahiti for a week. They chose the tiny island of Moorea with a population of only eight thousand at the time. Brown sent Ron Wallace a postcard to say he took the trip so he could become inspired for his next album.

During their trip to the Polynesian country, a seemingly insignificant event would illuminate the path that Brown's life would take next.

"While vacationing in Tahiti, I found an old copy of Sidney Sheldon's *Doomsday Conspiracy* on the beach," he said later. "I read the first page and then the next, and then the next. Several hours later, I finished the book and thought, 'Hey, I can do that.'"

And so, in one afternoon, the seed was planted, though it would take a couple more years until the first significant sprout would appear.

■ ■ ■

In his time away from Exeter, Brown had learned a lot about life. He had also discovered a few things—from Professor Lelchuk at Amherst and the art history class at the University of Seville— that had opened his eyes.

He was thrilled to be finally going home. He missed New England, and he had never gotten used to living in Los Angeles anyway.

Best of all, the love of his life was coming with him. Paul Zollo always thought that they complemented each other very well. "Dan was a very warm, likable guy," said Zollo. "He was very friendly and complimentary about my work. Blythe's greatest aspect was her sense of humor. She liked to laugh, she liked jokes, and she laughed heartily when she heard one that struck her."

As Brown had already seen, Blythe wholeheartedly supported his dreams and vowed to do whatever it would take for him to reach them. Just as she had done in her job at the Academy, she was content to stay behind the scenes and provide support while he actively pursued a creative career. "I always found her support of and her belief in Dan to be touching and rare," said Zollo.

As the couple stepped off the plane and headed for Exeter, Brown couldn't wait to see how it looked through his new eyes.

CHAPTER THREE

PLOTTING THE FUTURE

ONCE BROWN WAS back on his home turf with the people and culture he knew and understood, he felt he could breathe again.

Before leaving California, Brown had lined up a teaching job at his alma mater, Phillips Exeter Academy. Though he enjoyed teaching at Beverly Hills Prep, he knew it would feel much different at the Academy. His memories of Phillips Exeter were warm ones, both from when he lived on campus with his family during his boyhood and from when he was a full-time student. Brown would be teaching English classes, both literature and writing, and he would assign to his students classics like *The Iliad* and *Of Mice and Men*, Shakespeare and Dostoyevsky. To supplement his income, he also taught Spanish to seventh-graders at the Lincoln Akerman School in nearby Hampton Falls. He bicycled between the two schools in good weather and bad.

Since he wouldn't need to wear anything fancier than a tweed blazer or sport jacket in the classroom, Brown gave away a few old suits to his colleague Paul Zollo. Brown knew that his soon-to-be former coworker often wore old-fashioned suit jackets to the office. "I felt funny about it, as if he considered me somewhat of a charity case," said Zollo, "but I accepted them anyway." Brown had been regularly teased in Hollywood about his wardrobe, so perhaps he thought that leaving the suits behind meant he could leave his old life there as well.

Brown was flying high from the sale of *187 Men to Avoid*. When he and Blythe first kicked around the idea for the book, based on the ludicrous characters and dating and mating methods of the men and women they had witnessed in Los Angeles, they figured that with the skills Blythe had honed working at the National Academy of Songwriters, she was perfectly capable of selling the book idea to a publisher.

Once they came up with the complete title—*187 Men to Avoid: A Survival Guide for the Romantically Frustrated Woman*—the Danielle Brown pseudonym followed, since the content and topic of the book virtually dictated that the author be female.

Editor Elizabeth Beier acquired the book for Berkley Books in New York, now part of the Penguin Group, and scheduled the book for publication in August 1995. From the back cover: "Keep away. Far, far away. Because when a woman is hunting for the love of a lifetime, she has to know what species to look out for. Here's an essential field guide to 187 men to avoid . . . stinging insects, dangerous parasites, and vermin of every kind." But perhaps the two most intriguing entries in the book are "Men who write self-help books for women," and the last item in the book: "Men who read women's books (like this one)."

After all, the copyright holder is listed in the book as Dan Brown, and the book itself is an abbreviated self-help book for women; Blythe's name is nowhere in the book. The "About the Author" description reads, "Danielle Brown currently lives in New England: teaching school, writing books, and avoiding men."

As is the case with most quirky humor books, when the book came out, the publisher sent out a couple hundred press releases to promote it. Both Blythe and Dan were surprised that the publisher didn't do more to get the word out about the book, but they chalked it up to experience. The book sold a few thousand copies before going out of print. Brown would later acknowledge that he had written a book prior to *Digital Fortress*, but only if a reporter brought it up first. All he would say about *187 Men to Avoid* was, "It was a silly little humor book whose title will forever remain a secret. The book is now out of print, and rightly so."

In between teaching and working on the book, in 1993, Brown continued work on his CD in progress, *Angels & Demons*. After the poor showing of his debut CD, he knew he had to do everything himself, and he relished the project. He had become aware of the Gothic-inspired artwork of artist John Langdon, who specialized in creating ambigrams, words written in a graphic form that can be read right side up and upside down. Brown thought this style of art would be perfect for the cover.

The *Angels & Demons* CD came out in 1995 and contained a song that Brown has maintained was performed at the 1996 Olympics, "Peace in Our Time." Some of his critics would later point to the fact that the song doesn't appear on the official collection of songs featured at the Olympics as proof that Brown stretches the facts when it serves a purpose, but the truth is that the CD doesn't include all of the songs that were performed at not only the opening and closing ceremonies but also at countless events during the two weeks of the event.

In any case, the fact that Brown chose this particular title—"Peace in Our Time"—is an early indication of his interest in merging significant historical issues and events with modern-day concerns. The title of the song is based on a quote from British Prime Minister Neville Chamberlain, who said he had secured "peace in our time" after signing the Munich Pact with German Chancellor Adolf Hitler in 1938. The Pact essentially allowed Hitler to invade Czechoslovakia, and World War II started approximately one year later.

Although *Dan Brown* and *Angels & Demons* were produced only two years apart, the differences in the two albums are striking. They underscore how the amount of money spent on production becomes glaringly evident in the quality of the sound and the overall package.

While *Dan Brown* featured performances by some of the best studio musicians in Los Angeles and contained a ten-page stapled CD insert with several photographs, *Angels & Demons* came with a three-panel fold-out insert with no art, aside from John Langdon's ambigram on the front cover. Instead of top-name, top-dollar professional musicians, Brown relied mostly on his synthesizer and several friends who played violin, mandolin, and saxophone to add acoustic accents where he deemed them necessary. Further, *Dan Brown* featured a team of professional backup singers, but *Angels & Demons* had only one: Blythe. On his first CD, Dan Brown was listed as the sole composer and lyricist on the songs, but he shared production credits with Barry Fasman, who took full credit for the musical arrangements. On *Angels & Demons*, the credit line reads, "Written, arranged, and produced by Dan Brown."

It's almost humorous that while he thanked Steinway Pianos in the liner notes for his debut, in *Angels & Demons* he thanks Digidesign, a company that produced ProTools, the most advanced synthesized music software available at the time, and Macintosh Computers. He also acknowledged "the ingenious John Langdon for attempting and accomplishing the impossible." And he thanked Blythe not once but twice: "for being my tireless cowriter, coproducer, second engineer, significant other, and therapist."

On *Angels & Demons*, his voice is not as prominently featured as it was on *Dan Brown*. He was more of a crooner on the debut, and his voice sounds higher and smoother on the second album. Part of this, of course, is due to the radically scaled-down equipment he had to use. But his lyrics are far more biting and pessimistic—and soul-searching—on *Angels & Demons* than the songs on his debut album.

They also clearly point to his disillusionment with his experience making the debut CD. On "Here in These Fields," composed in the three-quarter time of a waltz, he reports:

I have returned
With the lessons I've learned
Three thousand miles away.

The song is a pleasant sailor's ditty with rollicking piano arpeggios throughout, and Brown's voice is well-suited to this song: It's strong and contains more emotion than any of the songs on his previous album. In fact, the tone on *Angels & Demons* is completely different from his eponymous CD. For one, he's already won the love of his life, and his songwriting clearly reflects this. The lyrics in each song are less modern, and thankfully, there is no song about phone sex or S&M anywhere on the album.

The lyrics he's written for "Beat of My Heart," a slow, reflective song, make it clear that he was glad to put his musical career behind him: "I've taken direction for my last time/ You feel yourself slipping away." He vows to remain true to himself from this point on.

"Peace in Our Time," the last song on the album, offers up a curious line in which he implores the listener to "weigh your ambition against your youth," perhaps as a caution to those who choose to move away from their home to seek riches that can be found right where they started.

It's not clear how his experience in Hollywood affected his religious faith, but in the song "All I Believe," it sounds like he no longer places much stock in religion.

I don't need a preacher
To save me
From demons

Just like the previous album, he uses the words *angel* or *demon* and other religious imagery in most of the songs. Also echoing his earlier effort, Brown reveals his educational background by occasionally throwing in a word that would send most people to a dictionary. In "Where Are the Heroes," a couple of phrases include "purloined hearts" and "the coffers leak."

Perhaps most revealing, however, is that while eight of the ten songs on *Dan Brown* could be considered love songs, none appear on *Angels & Demons*. "All I Believe" comes closest despite its anti-religious fervor:

> *And I kneel down to pray*
> *But your name*
> *Is all I can say.*

Of course, the title song on Dan Brown's second CD is the most intriguing because he would later use the same title for his second novel, in which Robert Langdon would make his debut. In the title track, Brown sings about the angels and demons that call to him every day, and the fact that he can't tell them apart. It almost sounds like he wrote the lyrics at a time in his life when his agnostic, scientific side was battling it out with his spiritual side, and he was still unsure which one would win out. Here are the first lines:

> *Angels and demons*
> *Speak my name*
> *They sing to me at night*

In the song "Where Are the Heroes," the lyrics foreshadow Brown's later efforts to create a literary hero of his own, in the form of Robert Langdon:

> *Where are the heroes now*
> *This kingdom's burning fast*
> *The castle walls will never last*

"Where Are the Heroes" starts off as a ballad, and then develops into a complaint about modern society. It recalls a past time when honor and bravery were king, compared to today, when we live in a world where "every man has got his price."

The *Angels & Demons* CD would be Brown's swan song in the music business. He had given it his all, but he was unwilling to bend to music industry conventions for success. Now it was time to turn away from music and focus his creative energy solely on writing. And with the help and support of Blythe—who became his wife after they left California in a wedding ceremony near North Conway, New Hampshire, where he had spent his summers as a child—Brown felt he could do anything.

■ ■ ■

The year 1995 was a turning point in the life of Dan Brown. His first book, *187 Men to Avoid*, was published and his last CD, *Angels & Demons*, was released. More important, however, he began to write his first novel, which would serve as the springboard that would eventually lead to *The Da Vinci Code*. The idea that led him there essentially fell into his lap.

One morning in the spring of 1995, two Secret Service agents unexpectedly showed up on the Phillips Exeter campus. After flashing their credentials, they told the headmaster they wanted to talk to a particular student, claiming he was a threat to national security. Of course, word spread like wildfire throughout the school, as students and teachers wondered what the kid had done.

As it turned out, the boy had been online on a school computer the previous night sending e-mails to a friend complaining about the state of the nation's politics. He e-mailed his friend that he was so mad at President Bill Clinton that he wanted to kill him, and the Secret Service paid a visit to make sure he wasn't serious. The student said he was only kidding, and nothing more came of it.

When Brown learned the full details of the incident, however, he was surprised to discover that the United States government not only had the ability to monitor the e-mail messages of its citizens, as well as other forms of electronic communication like cell phone calls, but that it was doing just that. Despite the fact the agency had attempted to recruit his father, Brown has said this is when he first learned of the existence of the National Security Agency, a government organization empowered to use covert means to detect plots against the government before they happen.

"My first reaction was kind of the gut reaction everybody has, which is, 'Hey, these guys are invading my privacy,'" he said.

"I couldn't help wondering how the Secret Service had isolated this one message from the countless millions on the Internet," he said. "When I stumbled on the truth, I knew I had to write about it."

That "truth" turned out to be what is known as a "sniffer" program, software that can detect words in e-mail and other electronic communications. By themselves, the words may appear to be innocuous, but when they appear in the same sentence they can prove to be highly lethal. "The NSA's supercomputers scan e-mail and other digital communiqués looking for dangerous word combinations like *kill* and *Clinton* in the same sentence," he explained, which is how the agency showed up on campus to interrogate the student. Even though e-mail traffic in 1995 was a fraction of what it was ten years later and sniffer programs were quite rudimentary at the time, Brown was able to determine certain facts about how the NSA traced the offensive e-mail to Phillips Exeter.

He figured that the NSA had put a sniffer on the server that handled all the e-mail originating at the private school. Of course, most e-mail servers also process messages that travel through other servers, so it's possible that the government was keeping its eye on someone else who was deliberately routing e-mail messages through the school's server in order to escape detection.

In any case, the incident stuck with Brown, and he was fascinated by the implications, as well as the fictional possibilities. He began to research the National Security Agency in depth and discovered that it served as the home of the most talented eavesdroppers in the United States. He described it this way: "The agency functions like an enormous vacuum cleaner that sucks in intelligence data from around the globe and processes it for subversive material," he said. He admitted that the more he learned about what was then a little-known agency and the moral issues revolving around national security and civilian privacy, the more he realized it would make a great backdrop for a novel. That's when he started to form the ideas that would become *Digital Fortress*.

The subject matter appealed to him not only because it involved elaborate codes and cryptography, but also because the NSA was itself essentially a secret society, albeit one with 25,000 employees. It was perhaps the most secret one he had encountered up to that point in his life. It was compelling enough for him to spend what little free time he had between his two teaching jobs researching and writing what would become his first novel.

He read many books about cryptography and the advanced technology employed at the NSA. He soon realized that the hardest part of his research would be sorting through the technical jargon. He wanted to present the information simply enough that a non-technical reader could understand, without bogging down the plot.

He turned to Usenet groups, essentially public discussion arenas specializing in a particular topic where enthusiasts of, say, golden retrievers, Cadillacs, or zithers could post questions to an online bulletin board and receive answers and feedback from like-minded enthusiasts. Brown has said that he relied on Usenet groups to ask questions pertinent to his research, and in some cases these initial queries developed into close friendships later on.

"Most cryptography was over my head; it was very complex," he admitted. "So I started posting specific questions on cryptography newsgroups on the Internet. The cryptographers started coming out of the woodwork and answering my questions." They also helped him sort through a lot of recently declassified data through the Freedom of Information Act. Many of his correspondents happened to be former employees of the NSA.

Brown's questions and their responses flew back and forth via anonymous e-mail servers to ensure the privacy of each person. These e-mails were not encrypted on either end, since encrypted e-mails were usually automatically tagged for analysis by the NSA. It was correctly assumed that anyone who knew enough to encrypt e-mail in those days of comparatively light e-mail traffic knew the United States government was watching. In any case, Brown found that his anonymous sources provided him with the basics, "but the second you reach this threshold past which things are classified, they don't even joke about it."

Once he came up with the idea for *Digital Fortress*, he began to get up at four in the morning to work on the novel before leaving for his teaching job at Phillips Exeter. At first, he started to write first thing in the morning out of necessity, because that was the only free chunk of time he had in the day.

But he soon discovered that writing early in the morning had clear advantages. "If I'm not at my desk by four or four-thirty in the morning, in my view, I've really missed the finest, most creative hours of the day," he said.

"A wonderful thing happens when you sleep and your mind is very, very creative. I wake up ready to write with a lot of ideas," he said. He also kept the ideas flowing through hours of writing with a couple of unusual tools. An antique hourglass on his desk reminds him when to take a break. When the last grains of sand have spilled into the lower glass chamber, he knows it's time to do some quick pushups and sit-ups, which also keep his blood pressure from falling too far. He sometimes uses quick exercises to break through writer's block.

The other tool he started to use was probably a holdover from his Los Angeles days: a set of gravity boots that look straight out of the 1980 Richard Gere movie *American Gigolo*. If the pushups and sit-ups don't do the trick, then he climbs onto a rack and hangs upside down for five or ten minutes.

"It's essentially a way to invert yourself and hang upside down like a bat," he explained. "It increases the blood flow to the head, and in my case, just lets me view the world in a slightly different perspective. And often, I will solve impossible problems while hanging upside down. But it is a little strange," he admitted.

With the kind of tight plotting that *Digital Fortress* and his later novels hinged on, it's easy to sense that Brown wouldn't have even thought about writing a novel while living in Los Angeles. "Writing requires a certain amount of introspection, solitude, and quiet," he said. "I don't know how people write in New York City."

Besides writing first thing in the morning, Brown also got into the habit of meticulously planning every plot point and twist, each character's relationship with the others, and the forward movement of the story before he wrote even one word of the novel. He realized that the more he knew about the story and its direction in advance, the better. Specifically detailing the tension from one chapter to the next was a great help when the time came for him to actually start writing.

"The stories are very intricate and plot-driven," he said. "They have a lot of twists, a lot of codes, and lots of surprises. You can't write those freehand. Those come from careful planning."

He knew that some novelists wrote blindly, by starting with an idea or image and then writing to see where it would take them. In literary works where the pace moves slowly and tension isn't integral to the plot, Brown could understand this. But the kind of story he wanted to write depended on building lots of suspense, keeping the reader guessing what would happen next, and throwing in lots of surprises—in other words, a page-turning novel. In Brown's view, those things just didn't happen; you had to plan for them.

With *Digital Fortress*, Brown also got into the habit of spending so much time researching his subject and characters that he ended up with easily three times the information needed to tell the story. With the help of Blythe's keen editing eye, the material that made it to the final draft was only the tip of the iceberg. But what went unsaid made the characters deeper and the story line richer in the end.

There was another reason he tended to over-research. He never knew which little nugget he'd uncover in a book, journal article, or conversation with an expert that he could base the entire puzzle of the novel on—the one obscure or shocking fact that would cause everything else to effortlessly fall into place.

Dan Brown liked to say that he began his research for each of his novels as a skeptic and ended up a believer. This process started with *Digital Fortress*. When he first began his research, he was shocked at the massive invasion of privacy he felt the NSA was conducting on a daily basis, and he said as much to a former cryptographer at the agency during an interview. Brown ceded that the man's response was to send him a document that showed that this "invasion of privacy" had prevented almost one terrorist attack a day in 1994 alone.

As he delved deeper into his research, Brown found that his own core set of values was beginning to change. "Every new technology that hits the market is a double-edged sword," he said. "The medical breakthroughs that can eradicate disease—genetic research, for example—if misused, can bring about the end of the human race. The question is not whether or not science will expand to meet man's growing needs, but whether man's philosophy will mature fast enough that we can truly comprehend our new power and the responsibility that comes with it."

He also learned an important distinction that is clear throughout *Digital Fortress*: The NSA essentially works to protect the safety of American citizens in the same way a parent protects a child. When he received the lists of attacks that the NSA had thwarted by invading our privacy, he admitted it was better that we not know about the disasters that almost happened. "It's

important to remember about terrorists that their job is not necessarily to kill people, it's to create terror," he said. "In the event
there is a bomb in New York City that NSA is able to stop with
three seconds left, they will make that bomb disappear and hope
nobody ever found out about it. Because whether or not the
bomb goes off, the second you know it almost went off, it's almost
as scary. So there is a lot of protecting our ignorance and inno-
cence," he said, admitting that this wasn't necessarily a bad thing.

Despite the fact that the subject matter thrilled him and he
was learning lots of new information about a topic that appealed
to him on two fronts—breaking codes and infiltrating a secret
society—Brown sometimes found the writing and researching a
tough slog, especially during the long days that began in front of
the computer at four in the morning.

"The toughest part was believing in the story even when
things were going badly, and forcing myself to spend anywhere
from five to eight hours a day on the manuscript even when I
wasn't positive I could make it work," he said. And there were
signs that Jack Heath's words—"Simpler is better"—hadn't quite
sunken in from freshman English class. "I did make it work, and
I'm glad I stuck with it, but I estimate I wrote over 1,000 pages to
end up with this 350-page novel."

Perhaps one thing that kept him going—and provided him
with some mild amusement during the long hours in front of a
blank computer screen—was the practice of naming characters
after past and present students and faculty at Phillips Exeter
Academy. In some cases he used the real names while, for others,
he turned them into anagrams or altered them in some other way.

While he borrowed from former colleagues to name his
characters, he largely avoided the work of other writers when he
began to work on a book. He says the novelists Jeffrey Archer,
Robert Ludlum, and Sidney Sheldon have influenced his writing,
but he chooses not to read their work—or any fiction, in fact—
when actively working on a book.

"I know I am supposed to name all the great writers who have inspired me, but I'm ashamed to say that I am so busy writing I have almost no time to read anything other than nonfiction and research books," he said. "On vacations I grab some mainstream thriller off the best-seller rack. Not glamorous, I know, but the truth."

But there's another reason he shies away from reading current popular fiction. "I read almost exclusively nonfiction, because I am always researching the next novel, but I don't like to read fiction when I'm writing because it tends to color what I am doing," he said. "When I do read a novel, only two or three a year, it is usually something mainstream and escapist."

He has admitted that teaching English and literature helped to prepare him for being an author. "I suppose discussing books in the classroom also helps me to analyze good fiction and incorporate similar themes into my own work," he said.

■ ■ ■

In the spring of 1996, after working on *Digital Fortress* for about a year, he and Blythe felt the novel was good enough to submit to an agent. After he had finished, Dan Brown had learned two things about the work of writing a novel.

First, he did not want to write one on spec again—that is, without the firm commitment of a publisher. And second, he didn't want to juggle writing while working two jobs. After several heartfelt discussions, he and Blythe decided that he would quit his teaching jobs in order to take a stab at writing full time. He left his full-time position at Phillips Exeter in June 1996 even though he hadn't yet sold *Digital Fortress* or even convinced a literary agent to represent him.

Blythe had sold *187 Men to Avoid* to Berkley Books back in 1993, but when the time came to interest a publisher in Dan's first novel, they both realized they needed someone who had more experience in the publishing industry, especially since he wanted to have a full-time career as a novelist. The world of publishing had changed to some degree in the three years since she sold *187 Men to Avoid*. Many publishers that had previously accepted proposals and manuscripts sent to them directly from unknown writers had closed their doors to unsolicited submissions. The "slush pile," as it was known, had become too unwieldy for publishers and a real drain on an editor's time. In 1996, most publishers had changed their policies to accept submissions only from literary agents.

And so they began the search for a literary agent. After receiving a copy of the manuscript, Olga and George Wieser, who ran a small literary agency called Wieser and Wieser, liked what they read and offered to submit the book to publishers. George and Olga had started their agency in 1975, and they had developed a specialty in adventure and military fiction, launching the career of novelist Dale Brown—no relation to Dan Brown—among others. Colleague Jake Elwell was named a partner in the agency in 1998 and later became president after George died in 1999.

Apparently George Wieser had a knack for spotting great talent early on. As the East Coast story editor for Paramount Pictures he purchased film rights to *The Godfather* by Mario Puzo based on only an outline and a few sample chapters.

George sold *Digital Fortress* to the Thomas Dunne Books imprint at St. Martin's Press three weeks after they first sent out the manuscript, but sadly, it was the last novel he sold before he was struck with cancer that would become fatal. Dunne then passed it along to editor Melissa Jacobs.

"I was exceptionally lucky. The first editor who saw it bought it," said Brown. "Part of it had to do with the fact that Internet security and privacy issues were exceptionally commercial at that time, and also that *Digital Fortress* was a piece of fiction that had actual ties to the real world."

He and Blythe were ecstatic. Friends had expressed doubts when he announced he was going to leave his teaching job before he had sold his first novel, and Dan and his wife viewed the sale as a confirmation that they had made the right decision.

In the wake of the novel's sale, Blythe decided to see what it felt like to be a published author herself. Or perhaps now that Dan's career as a novelist was taking off, being associated with a cheesy little novelty book would only detract from his goal of making a living writing fiction. Plus, bringing Danielle Brown back for a return engagement would be a bit too obvious, given that the copyright on that book was held by one Dan Brown for the whole world to see.

So they both decided that this time Blythe would serve as the author of another mercifully short humor book that again focused on one of the not-so-savory sides of men. However, *The Bald Book* was more complimentary than *187 Men to Avoid*; indeed, the Browns' sophomore effort in this category could rightfully be considered to be a love letter to bald men everywhere, with such positive pithy examples as "Your kissable surface area is increasing," "No more expensive hair products," and "No more cowlicks."

Agent Jake Elwell at Wieser and Wieser sold *The Bald Book* to Paul Dinas, who acquired it for Pinnacle Books, and it was published on June 1, 1998, four months after *Digital Fortress* came out.

The dedication read, "To my husband: Remember the immortal words of Francois Maynard: Look fearlessly on the end of things. Look into your mirror with contented gaze."

The author bio said, "Artist Blythe Brown lives in New England and spends her days painting while her husband happily goes bald."

Bio and copyright aside, "Dan was the writer of these [humor] books," said Elwell. "I'm not sure what Blythe contributed, aside from the drawings." The existence of Brown's early works is something that few people inside or out of the industry have known, and has never before been publicized. Indeed, whenever a reporter has asked him about the two novelty books,

Dan starts to act embarrassed and quickly changes the subject. He has never mentioned his authorship of them in any of his biographical notes or the press that has subsequently appeared for his thrillers.

■ ■ ■

Even though he had been toying around with a few ideas, Brown didn't feel he could proceed on a new novel until he knew the fate of his first one. After *Digital Fortress* sold, however, Brown felt comfortable going full speed ahead. He began to research his second novel, which he knew would be set primarily in Europe. He also knew the plot would revolve around art, as his interest in the subject had been rekindled since he met and married Blythe. While part of *Digital Fortress* was set in Seville, the medieval Spanish city served more as background than as an important part of the story. In his second novel, Brown knew that Rome, the city he picked, would have a starring role.

He continued to write at four in the morning, but by this time, he had moved his office out of the house and rented a small apartment on Water Street, a few blocks from his home. Brown's workspace is deliberately low-tech, with no phone or e-mail access, an arrangement that forces him to concentrate on nothing but his current novel-in-progress.

He spent the first year after *Digital Fortress* sold researching his second novel, which he tentatively titled *Angels & Demons*. He hadn't yet fleshed out the story or how the novel would unfold, but he knew it would involve the Vatican. He soon discovered writing full time was different from writing while working two jobs. He liked the opportunity to become completely immersed in the research, instead of squeezing it into an already packed day.

As before, Brown turned to the Internet for preliminary research on *Angels & Demons* and to get clarification on facts he was unclear about. He again relied on Usenet groups to post specific questions.

He would post the same query to numerous groups. About half the time, he would receive no response. Other times, he would receive a couple of polite explanations. Sometimes, however, his queries would spark an entire flame war online.

During this time, he and Blythe made the first of several trips to Europe to research his novel-in-progress. As was the case with *Digital Fortress,* a seemingly insignificant incident sparked the idea for *Angels & Demons.*

He and Blythe were on a tour of Vatican City—actually underneath it in a tunnel known as *Il Passetto,* a hidden underground passage that was intended to be used by the pope in case the Vatican was attacked. The guide leading the tour offhandedly mentioned that the Vatican's worst enemy in its history was a group known as the Illuminati, which he described as a group of scientists that threatened retribution against the pope in the seventeenth century for the punishment the Vatican meted out to Galileo, Copernicus, and other victimized scientists of the day.

The tour guide added that there were those who believed that the Illuminati was still around today—despite the fact that many scholars thought the group was long extinct—and that the cult had strong influences in political circles around the world.

The entire recitation probably took all of thirty seconds, but in that moment Brown knew his next novel would revolve around the theory that the guide's casually tossed-off remarks were true.

On that same trip, Brown was privileged to be granted an audience with Pope John Paul II, though he half dismisses the apparent grandeur of the meeting. "The term *audience* can be misleading," he said. "I did not sit down and have tea with the man." He describes the occasion as a "semi-private audience" in which the pope spent about thirty minutes with a group of visitors. Toward the end, the pope prayed with the guests and then blessed them. Brown recalled that he initially thought it was peculiar when Swiss Guards frisked each visitor before entering the special room for the audience. While they would have been able to detect any weapons, their primary objective was to catch someone carrying a hidden bottle of water.

"I later learned that any water present in the room when the pope said a blessing instantly becomes holy water, and the church did not want any of us taking holy water outside of Vatican City and trying to sell it," he noted.

"The most secure area that we saw was the necropolis, and only eleven people a day are allowed in to see it," he said. "It was absolutely really memorable and special." He did not get into the Vatican secret archives, as only three Americans in history are known to have been allowed inside; two of them were cardinals and one was a professor of religious studies. "I was allowed inside the Vatican library and the archives, not the secret archives," he said. When he was later asked, after *Angels & Demons* and *The Da Vinci Code* were published, if he thought he'd be granted access in the future, he drolly replied, "Chances are slim."

■ ■ ■

After learning the craft of constructing and writing a novel—one that was actually sold to a major New York publisher—Brown felt he had developed a good sense of what worked and what didn't when it came to commercial fiction. Setting, for one, was crucial. In fact, he would later affirm that choosing the setting for every novel he would write was almost as important as selecting the plot and characters. For his novels, he believed that location was perhaps the most important factor, since it would dictate the degree to which secrets could be revealed and present a unique opportunity to educate the reader about a topic they may know little about.

"If you're writing a love story, don't set it in the middle of a parking lot," he said, suggesting that the story be based in a location that is interesting all by itself. Once that is confirmed, he added, it's imperative to show the environment from a fly-on-the-wall perspective. "If you set a story in a private school and don't reveal any inside information about what it's like to work or study at a private school, then you've got a boring setting," he said.

Once he completed the writing of *Digital Fortress*, he realized that his first novel would be the only one to feature its characters Susan Fletcher and David Becker. He knew he wanted to work with new characters with more flexibility. Though he wasn't thinking about a character that could carry a series, he was aware that his next work of fiction would involve a romance in some way, as did *Digital Fortress*.

"I'm far more of a romantic than I am a political junkie," he said. "Romance, particularly when lovers are separated by insurmountable obstacles, always makes me care more about the characters, and therefore the action," he later said. "I am constantly trying to remind myself that readers read fiction to find out what happens to characters, not necessarily to get a travel guide of Paris or some religious, historical tome."

During the research for *Digital Fortress*, Brown knew how to get in touch with experts who would be willing to answer his questions and clarify certain points for him. Finding and selecting the experts he could rely on for *Angels & Demons*, however, was not as easy. He knew he couldn't just send an e-mail to a higher-up at the Vatican.

So he asked one of the cryptographer sources on his first novel if he knew anyone who was particularly good at researching esoteric data involving the Vatican. The source recommended Stan Planton, the head librarian at Ohio University-Chillicothe. Brown thought that sounded like a good idea, since when he was teaching at Phillips Exeter, he had often relied on Jacquelyn Thomas, the librarian at the Academy, when he would get stuck.

And so the two struck up an e-mail correspondence, which continued because, although Brown had other researchers helping him on his later novels, Planton tended to respond more quickly to his research requests. In addition, Planton often suggested obscure books and texts that other researchers would overlook.

"I know where to look, I'm a librarian," said Planton. "A lot of what I've done is simply say, 'Dan, you need to look in this particular book. I seldom provide him with a full text, just tell him where to look."

The librarian said that Brown's first requests revolved around facts and history about the Vatican, such as whether a pope had ever been murdered. When asked if he thought it was unusual that he would help a complete stranger with one novel under his belt who lived several states away, and whom he had never met face-to-face, Planton said he wished he could serve as a resource for more people, whether or not they're writers. "The message I want to convey is about the role of librarians these days," he said. "We're not just sitting in front of the stacks saying 'Shh.' If someone comes in with a legitimate project, we'll help."

After a year of solid research, Dan Brown completed most of his preliminary work. He had decided to continue his habit of beginning to work on a novel by doing nothing but research, then developing and fine-tuning an outline for the novel, and finally, proceeding to write the manuscript. While he loved being in research mode, he was doing exactly what he said he didn't want to do: working on another novel without a publisher's commitment. However, with the official publication date of *Digital Fortress* eighteen months in the future from the time it sold and with no other responsibilities on his plate, he and Blythe decided he should revel in the sheer luxury of having the time to do nothing but write. He could at least act like he was a full-time novelist, even though he wasn't getting paid.

Brown wrote *Digital Fortress* while juggling two teaching jobs, so it's obvious he's the kind of person who is more focused and efficient the more he has on his plate. The downside is that once he quit his teaching job in order to write fiction full-time, time seemed to expand and he experienced the first real trial of his writing career.

In the fall of 1997, he was looking forward to the publication of *Digital Fortress* a few months down the road. He was squarely in the last and, it seemed, his least favorite stage of work on *Angels & Demons*: the actual writing. After a promising start, he hit a brick wall. While he enjoyed every minute of doing the research, he simply did not want to sit down and write the novel.

"No amount of willpower—and I have a lot—could get me to sit in front of the computer," he said. "I welcomed absolutely any excuse to do something else, and I actually fantasized about searching for a mundane nine-to-five job that would save me from the life of having to be a writer." One day, he decided to procrastinate by driving to Boston for a demonstration of a new computer program known as voice recognition software, in which the user speaks into a tiny microphone and the program automatically converts the spoken word into written word.

"I am not one who places a lot of stake in technology," he admitted, which is surprising considering all the months of research and writing that he put into *Digital Fortress*. However, after testing out the software, Brown said it totally changed his outlook on writing, along with his motivation. "I am now communicating my ideas in a whole new way, and my writing feels totally fresh," he said. "I can pace the room as I write and stare off into space as I create dialogue. Writing feels exciting again."

Once Brown overcame his writer's block, he was able to continue working on *Angels & Demons* without a hitch. With the publication of his second novel still a few months away, he again turned to Usenet groups online. He started to correspond with other published writers to exchange advice and ideas as well as moral support. He wanted to see what they experienced when their first novels were published so he could have some idea of what to expect when *Digital Fortress* came out.

Often, the conversation turned to what publishers do to market the novels they publish, but mostly what they don't do. It didn't take long for Brown to get a sense that he'd have to do most of the work publicizing his book if he wanted it to be a success. He offered his take on the topic by mentioning a *Wall Street Journal* article about a novelist who was so unhappy with the lack of marketing attention from his publisher that the writer spent $35,000 of his own money to get the word out, which was many times the amount of the advance the author received for the novel.

But he also had an idea of the potential money that writing could bring him. In a message Brown posted to the alt.books.reviews Usenet group, he replied to another poster's earlier review of *Jaws* author Peter Benchley's novel *White Shark* to boast of his connection with the famous novelist and fellow Phillips Exeter alumnus, and to comment on the review.

"He is a terrific guy, very modest," wrote Brown, "and said something I thought you might appreciate. His quote was something along the lines of, 'By the time I realized I didn't know how to write, I was making too much money to stop!'"

Brown's decision to mention this specific quote would prove prophetic, at least among the more vociferous critics of *The Da Vinci Code*. But he clearly saw that it was possible to make money—and a lot of it—if he could figure out a precise formula and story line.

Even before he could rightfully claim to be a published novelist, Dan Brown was starting to see that there was more involved in becoming a full-time author than just writing a good story.

He just didn't know it would get much tougher before it got better.

CHAPTER **FOUR**

A FALSE START

DAN AND BLYTHE celebrated in February 1998 when *Digital Fortress* was published, exactly three years after he first came up with the idea for the novel.

Blythe took care of most of the publicity tasks for the novel, from writing press releases to booking her husband on talk shows and setting up interviews with newspaper reporters.

It was during this time that Brown got his first taste of what could rightfully be called the schizophrenic side of working as a career novelist. He was in the middle of writing *Angels & Demons* when he'd have to talk with reporters and producers to promote a book that he'd finished well over a year before. Some novelists take the dichotomy in stride, while others have a difficult time switching back and forth, especially if the setting and/or subject matter in both books are radically different. Indeed, some authors understandably stop all work on a novel-in-progress while promoting a newly published book.

This is how Dan Brown found himself discussing how an e-mail gets passed from one server to another and how the government spies on its citizens while he was actively analyzing Italian Renaissance sculptors and traveling the secret passageways under the Vatican, at least in his mind.

In trying to get Brown booked on shows where he could discuss the NSA and e-mail privacy, Blythe seemingly had her work cut out for her. Most novels are difficult—if not impossible—to promote to the media with press releases and other publicity materials. It's much easier to get the attention of the media by promoting a nonfiction book, particularly a how-to or other prescriptive nonfiction book, because then a publicist can market the title as a solution to a problem.

However, Blythe was able to promote *Digital Fortress* with little problem since the topic of the book was timely, and she was able to offer her husband as a source to advise readers and viewers on how to protect themselves online.

After all, in 1998, e-mail was still a somewhat new technology for many people who didn't understand its technical aspects or else didn't want to know. In either case, it was just a novelty and it worked. The publicity materials that Blythe developed focused on the scary aspects of what people didn't know about their e-mail. *Who's Reading Your E-mail?* and *Who's Watching You Online?* were two angles that made Dan Brown popular with reporters and producers. Some days, he would do four radio interviews a day to talk about *Digital Fortress*.

By giving interviews to any radio host or newspaper reporter Blythe could arrange, and signing books at almost every bookstore in New Hampshire (which makes them "nonreturnable" to the publisher in the consignment business of retail bookselling), Dan learned the ropes of book promotion. He and Blythe hoped that, if they were able to prove they could sell books on their own, maybe next time around the publisher would handle more of the workload.

Brown pulled out all the stops. He had learned from promoting his music that you never knew how someone could help you, so he prepared postcards with an image of the cover of the book on one side and reviews, comments, and a toll-free ordering number on the other. He also devised a succinct motto for the novel: "The government's greatest secret is that they know all of yours." He sent the cards to everyone he had ever known in the music business, as well as to his fellow classmates at Amherst College and Phillips Exeter.

Also stamped on the card—which was postmarked February 26, 1998—was "First printing sold out nationwide in nine days. Now back in stock." While this may sound impressive, St. Martin's is a studiously cost-conscious publisher, especially when it comes to first novelists. The first printing for *Digital Fortress* couldn't have been much more than a few thousand copies. In all fairness, though, the sales of other first novels may never warrant a second printing even after a year or two.

One of the reasons Brown was able to move so many copies, aside from the massive publicity push that Blythe designed and executed, was perhaps that he was extremely stingy with the free copies provided to friends and family. Granted, publishers typically don't give an author more than twenty free copies of their book, but Brown knew the only way to prove to St. Martin's that he was worth the goods was to help move books out the door. Brown's L.A. acquaintance Ron Wallace of Creative Musicians Coalition remembered that he was a little miffed that he had to pay full price for his copy—$24.95 plus $4 shipping—but at the same time he understood that at Dan's stage of the game, every copy counted.

As would happen later with *The Da Vinci Code*, soon after *Digital Fortress* was published, Brown began to receive correspondence from readers who pointed out errors and omissions about certain technical aspects he described in the novel.

But overall, at least in the beginning, Brown was very open to hearing from readers, whether it was to compliment him on his storytelling ability or to tell him about errors or oversights. In fact, on his Web site, he went out of his way to encourage this. He held a contest to invite visitors to decipher a puzzle that was tied in with the theme of the novel. In exchange, Brown would send a free autographed bookplate to those who had successfully cracked the code.

One of the reasons reader feedback to *Digital Fortress* came fast and furious was that Brown had set up a comprehensive Web site in order to promote the book. Though today having a Web site to promote yourself as a writer is virtually a given, even among modestly published authors, in 1998 authors regularly argued over the merits of having a Web site. The technology was still new and unproven, and many felt it wasn't necessary. Although the majority of American households owned a personal computer, many people still refrained from using the Internet, either because they didn't understand it or felt the amount of useful information out there at the time was negligible.

Since *Digital Fortress* specifically appealed to a reading audience who tended to be early adopters, or the first in line to buy new technological gadgets, designing a Web site with plenty of information and interactive features was a crucial way to gain their attention. At the very least, it would stand out as a rarity. That the book was also available as an e-book likewise contributed to the novel's early success.

Indeed, the Web site—www.digitalfortress.com—made the novel sound irresistible, with plenty of blurbs and testimonials from writers and experts in the field. John J. Nance, a top thriller author, wrote, "A disturbing, cutting-edge techno-thriller which should galvanize everyone who sends or receives e-mail or even dreams of navigating the Web. Dan Brown has unleashed a surprise . . . a gripping story on the frontier of cyberspace which adroitly explores the frighteningly delicate line between defending us and controlling us."

Don Ulsch, managing director of the National Security Institute, called the novel "Frighteningly real! A powerful and memorable novel. More intelligence secrets than Tom Clancy. *Digital Fortress* is closer to the truth than any of us dare imagine."

Brown also offered up several codes and challenged readers to break them. Here's one:

Can you break this code?
YAOROVSEUEETHNCS

He then provided a hint for those having a bit of trouble, informing the reader that the code borrows a page from Julius Caesar, adding that the ancient Roman emperor liked to employ a bit of whimsy when he introduced a puzzle to his subjects. Referred to today as a Caesar Box, Brown's code breakers were instructed simply to stack the letters in rows on top of each other, four letters to each line, so that the solution, when read vertically downward, would spell out a message that ties in perfectly with the theme of the novel:

YOU HAVE NO SECRETS.

He then offered two more codes to break, and if a reader solved all three puzzles and sent proof to Brown via e-mail, he'd send an autographed bookplate through the mail.

■ ■ ■

It shouldn't come as a surprise that early readers of *Digital Fortress* were geeks and technophiles, given the content of the novel. Two months after it was published, Brown appeared at the monthly meeting of the New Hampshire chapter of the American Society for Industrial Security, and Blythe arranged for a reporter from the state's largest daily newspaper, the *Union Leader*, to attend Dan's talk. Although he had already heard about some of the mistakes he made in the book from several readers via e-mail, this would be his first face-to-face meeting with readers who were bona fide experts in the field he had written about. And as it turned out, they clearly found fault with some of the "facts" he had presented in *Digital Fortress*.

John Pignato, chairman of the local ASIS chapter, whose résumé includes training agents for the NSA and working as a security consultant for federal buildings, was present at the meeting. He told Brown he had some issues with a few of the details in the book, and at first he begged off offering his opinion by explaining that he couldn't discuss them because it was classified information.

But he did eventually comment on one detail where Brown had erred concerning legal issues, specifically regarding due process and how court orders are issued, two points that were integral to the plot of *Digital Fortress*. Undoubtedly, other scientists who attended the meeting told Brown of other errors in the book. But they got lost in the muddle as soon as an audience member suggested that the author was likely under NSA surveillance because he was so visible in promoting the novel, since several news stories about Brown and *Digital Fortress* had been picked up by the Associated Press and distributed to newspapers nationwide.

At the talk, Brown didn't act too surprised at this bit of information. "I would be very surprised at this point if I was not under surveillance," he said. His anonymous NSA sources had already told him that based on the subject matter of his book, the federal agency had been keeping tabs on him for a while and that the government was probably tapping his phone. A few weeks after his ASIS talk, Brown admitted that the NSA had already extended him a "cordial" invitation to visit NSA headquarters. His anonymous contacts informed him that, à la Don Corleone, this was not the kind of offer anyone should refuse.

He also learned that being a published novelist can open up both author and book to some real nitpicky criticism. Some readers complained that the main characters in the story—Susan Fletcher, the beautiful genius cryptographer working at the NSA, and David Becker, the handsome professor at Georgetown University and foreign language expert—were larger than life. Brown deflected the criticism by likening the novel to those that he preferred to read when he opted for fiction, calling *Digital Fortress* a fun escapist story. "I personally enjoy reading about characters that have exceptional talents," he said. "We run into boring people all day long, so why not read about some interesting ones?"

On his Web site, Brown included links to innovative technology, in order to engage readers and to encourage them to order the book. He provided two maps of the NSA compound at Fort Meade as well as the floor plan for the NSA headquarters. He also included an article from CNN about a Pentagon report on upcoming spy devices, from microrobots to data mining and even digital "noses" that had the potential to replace drug-sniffing dogs. Brown was remarkably prescient, since many of these topics are still being debated today. He thought that it was precisely these kinds of behind-the-scene peeks that would attract curious readers who congregated in online chats and forums devoted to these subjects.

Another selection revealed that he was placing codes on the covers of his books from the very beginning. "A Carefully Hidden Clue: The plot of *Digital Fortress* revolves around the quest for a secret pass-key that will break an ingenious code and avert the biggest intelligence disaster in U.S. history. We've concealed a clue to this key in the author photo on the jacket flap."

He and Blythe also promoted *Digital Fortress* online through Usenet groups. Brown visited different groups, supposedly to ask questions. But it was sometimes transparent that the main purpose was to announce the publication of *Digital Fortress*. In those early days, online etiquette was still being hashed out and many newcomers to these online forums believed you could promote your new product—or novel—as long as you couched the message with some useful advice or asked a relevant question. It was very easy to come across as an opportunist and variation of a spammer in these cases, and Dan was guilty of committing Usenet faux pas that generated angry responses.

Here's one of his posts:

> *I am a St. Martin's Press author whose first novel*
> Digital Fortress *just sold out its first printing*

nationwide in only 9 days (before the official Feb. 9 pub. date.) A lot of people are now telling me to hang on to my first edition copies because they will be worth a lot due to the fast sell-through of the first run. I know nothing about book collecting and was hoping someone could tell me if this is true. Thanks much, Dan Brown, Author, Digital Fortress

And here's one of the early replies:

If you want to publicize the book then please be upfront about it. Honestly, what author would ask if he/she should "hang on" to their own work. Did you think that no one would notice your e-mail address starts with publicity@. . .

Subsequent posts contained advice on book collecting along with congratulations. Brown posted twice more to this thread, and some of his comments are eerily prophetic:

First:

Wow. Sorry if my message came across as otherwise; it was an honest request. A book collector from Framingham, Massachusetts, just came to our local bookstore and bought ten copies of my novel and then stopped by my home to have me sign them. I thought he was nuts. I am brand-new to this business and was trying to get some information from people like yourself who know about it. (I thought that's what groups like this were for.) As for the publicity address, it was my wife's computer. I am an unknown author, and don't have the luxury of a publicity staff. I'm sorry I offended you.

And then this:

> *Thank you so much for your generous response to my inquiry. I feel like I just got a crash course in book collecting! I now have four first editions on ice, and I guess we'll see what happens. Worse case scenario, I can use them for kindling some day. As per the requisites to make a book valuable, because I collect nothing myself I find it fascinating that a series of events can make certain very common objects more or less valuable over time. I certainly know nobody's buying the book for my name recognition!*

Sometimes, online promotion could backfire. A couple of readers he had sent advanced reading copies to then posted their own reviews. One in particular complimented Dan's use of plotting, but described—in what must have been overly excruciating detail for Dan—the technical errors that appeared in the book.

In any case, Brown was beginning to hit his stride, and he quickly discovered that he definitely preferred book publishing to the music business. The book stood on its own, and he didn't have to perform or change his persona. Doing media interviews was fine, since he spent most of the time talking about the book, and not his personal life. He was promoting a product, not himself, which meant he could keep himself out of the spotlight and focus it on the book instead.

■ ■ ■

Over the winter of 1998, between promoting *Digital Fortress* and writing *Angels & Demons*, neither Dan nor Blythe had a minute to breathe. But they quickly found the time when Gary Goldstein, an editor at the Pocket Books imprint at Simon & Schuster, called. Goldstein had read *Digital Fortress*, liked it, and asked Brown what he was working on next.

With the help of his agent, Jake Elwell, Brown sent Goldstein the two-hundred-page outline he had developed for *Angels & Demons*. Elwell negotiated a two-book deal for Brown: *Angels & Demons*, and a second untitled novel.

Contracts were signed, an advance check was sent, and Brown continued to work on the manuscript that would become his first thriller starring Robert Langdon, not forgetting the lessons he learned after *Digital Fortress* was published. Instead of accepting them at face value, he started double-checking "facts" he learned online, whether he read about them on Web sites or through e-mails in response to Usenet queries. He learned there was nothing like a book—the more obscure and difficult to find, the better, in some cases—that would allow him to ferret out wonderfully detailed information that would have been close to impossible to find elsewhere.

One example he cites of information he was able to locate only in a little-known book is the rituals cardinals are required to conduct when selecting a new pope. Of course, in the wake of the death of Pope John Paul II in 2005, millions of people around the world became familiar with the various ceremonies of the conclave, from burning the ballots after each vote to the colored smoke that emanates from the chimney to the simple meals that are served to the sequestered cardinals for the duration of the vote. In fact, many not-very-intrepid news reporters used the descriptions they had read in *Angels & Demons* as their primary resource for the specifics and secrets involved in the election of a new pope.

Brown found much of the rich details of the conclave in a book by a Jesuit scholar who had interviewed more than one hundred cardinals. "That was obviously something I never would have had the time or connections to do," he said.

■ ■ ■

As Brown hunkered down to work on his second novel and basked in the attention the media had been giving him for *Digital*

Fortress, The Bald Book was published on June 1, 1998, "just in time for Father's Day," as the publisher's promotional materials put it. As with *187 Men to Avoid*, the book enjoyed modest sales before sinking like a stone. Even though Blythe and Dan had learned legions about what it took to promote a book to the media and the public, the couple felt like there was no need to get the word out about this little humor book, now that it looked like Dan's dreams of becoming a novelist were coming true.

Just when everything finally seemed to be going right for Brown, a bomb hit. Gary Goldstein, the editor at Pocket Books who had enthusiastically offered Brown the contract, suddenly left the company. While this was far from an uncommon occurrence, it could easily doom any books that the departing editor had acquired, since the book's primary cheerleader was no longer around and, for the editor who ends up with the book in limbo, it's just another project to add to an already overwhelming workload. The publishing industry even has a word for such circumstances: Dan Brown's new novel at his new publishing house had become an "orphan."

In an industry where international conglomerates demand increased profits and stockholders demand higher stock prices, the ones caught in the vise of this once-genteel business are, more often than not, the editors who decide which books will appear on the shelves a year or two in the future. In many cases, an editor is only as good as her last book, and she can be marginalized or even fired for miscalculating on her titles. By the same token, if an editor senses that a couple of her personally acquired titles are likely to tank, she can beat feet to a new publisher before the red ink becomes too obvious. In other words, editorial departments at many publishers these days essentially have become a revolving door that spits out editors depending on their performance while siphoning in new recruits, many of whom are fleeing their own literary children at previous houses.

So halfway through his work schedule, Dan Brown and his novel-in-progress were orphaned. While some writers need constant hand-holding and gentle assurance while sweating out each word of their manuscripts, at the time Brown wasn't one of them. Instead, he relied heavily on the eye of his wife to point out inconsistencies and errors. So while he was disconcerted by the fact that he was currently a writer without an editor to anchor his book to the house—especially since he was still learning the intricacies and politics particular to publishing—Elwell told him to keep his head down and keep working, and to leave the worrying to him.

A couple of months later, Jason Kaufman arrived at Pocket Books, and Brown had a new editor. Kaufman was well-acquainted with the editorial revolving door of publishing; in the ten years he had spent in the industry up to that point, he had held five different jobs. A month after he had started working at the Simon & Schuster imprint, a higher-up made him responsible for overseeing the two books Brown was contractually obligated to write for the publisher.

As he continued to work on *Angels & Demons*, Brown focused on placing the codes he loved so much in just the right places within the novel. Because ambigrams were such a prominent feature in the book, he leaned on his editor to include an ambigram on the cover of the book. Fortunately, Brown already had one to hand to the cover designer: the ambigram John Langdon had created for the *Angels & Demons* CD he had released back in 1994. Brown also recommended that John Langdon design the ambigrams that would appear inside the book, to create some continuity.

Seasoned authors—and even those with only one book under their belts like Brown—quickly come to realize that once the manuscript has been handed in, their responsibilities to the production phase of publishing are over. Of course, he'd have to answer copyediting questions and check the galleys for typos, but typically only the art department and the sales force have the final say over the content and design of the cover.

Authors often pass along suggestions via an editor, but for the most part that advice proceeds no further than the editor's desk since the art and sales staff assume—correctly, most of the time—that writers live in the world of words and don't have a clue about what does and doesn't tempt a reader to pick up a book from a store display.

But *Angels & Demons* was different, because ambigrams were an integral part of the story. To both Brown and Kaufman, it seemed obvious one had to appear on the cover. However, the ambigram title appeared only on the first hardcover edition, though the ambigrams remained inside the book in all editions. Perhaps the sales department felt the title on the cover would be too difficult to read once it was reproduced on the smaller paperback. Or perhaps, when shrunken down to the thumbnail covers that appear in a publisher's backlist catalog, it would have just looked like an unreadable mess.

In any case, on subsequent reprints of the book, the ambigram title on the cover was replaced with a more traditional layout and design, though later on, as the runaway success of *The Da Vinci Code* accelerated, Dan Brown's name on the cover of *Angels & Demons* and his other two novels grew larger, eventually becoming the same size as the titles. This is a sign that an author has become a brand name—or, in the parlance of the publishing industry, a "franchise" author.

But Brown wasn't a franchise yet. His second novel was published in April 2000, and he decided that he had enough publishing experience under his belt that *Angels & Demons*, and his subsequent novels, would each sell more copies than the one before. He believed his new novels would widen his exposure, build his fan base, and spark interest in his older books.

At least, that was the way that writing commercial fiction was supposed to work, in theory. He would soon find out how very wrong he was.

CHAPTER FIVE

UNCERTAIN DAYS

THOUGH DAN BROWN had a new publisher for his second novel, the publicity efforts on behalf of the book were about the same as St. Martin's had been for *Digital Fortress*—which meant that, once again, Blythe turned on the publicity machine. The plot of *Angels & Demons* was not as timely as *Digital Fortress*, but Blythe and Dan soldiered on as before, taking charge of their own marketing and promotion to the media.

In an unexpected development, when *Angels & Demons* was published, it didn't take long for word to travel back that people were actually using the novel as a kind of tour book.

"There's a cybercafe in Rome somewhere near Bernini's famous Fountain of the Four Rivers, and it seems every other day some tourists have stopped in there to e-mail me," he said. "They say, 'I'm in this cybercafe and I have your book, and I followed all these statues and paintings and buildings, and you're right, they're all right where you said they were.'"

He was amused that readers were using his novel—a fictional adventure through Rome—as a substitute for a Fodor's travel guide. And so this became one of the angles Blythe used to promote the book.

As he talked to the media and readers about *Angels & Demons*, Brown was taken aback when some readers accused him of being anti-Catholic and an atheist, among other things. They also charged him with favoring science over religion, a point he always vehemently denied, having grown up in a household where the two sides—embodied in his parents—coexisted quite peacefully.

"In many ways, I see science and religion as the same thing," he said. "Both are manifestations of man's quest to understand the divine. Religion savors the questions while science savors the quest for answers. Science and religion seem to be two different languages attempting to tell the same story, and yet the battle between them has been raging for centuries and continues today."

Brown was now a writer with two published novels under his belt and a firm commitment from Simon & Schuster to publish at least one more. With each manuscript that he researched, wrote, and sweated over, he became more adept at plotting, writing, and planning the path a story would take.

As before, he toured the state of New Hampshire to appear at book signings for *Angels & Demons*. When unpublished writers approached him and asked for tips on finding an agent and publisher—which was beginning to occur more frequently—he cited advice he had read in a book called *Writing the Blockbuster Novel* by renowned literary agent Albert Zuckerman. He told them that none of that would be difficult if they paid attention to the structure and content of their novels in the first place.

Of course, he would never know how many of these aspiring novelists would take his advice to heart. Because the requests continued to come with great regularity, he finally decided to distill his advice into a detailed article on his Web site. This turned out to be quite a shrewd marketing move on Dan's part. In the article, he slyly suggested that in order to really see what he was talking about, it was essential to buy one—or all—of his novels.

His "Seven Powerful Tips"—which he credits the Albert Zuckerman book for teaching him—is no longer at the danbrown.com Web site in its original form. But the outline provides a revealing look at how he plans and crafts the flow of his own novels.

1. Setting, Setting, Setting: Expose your readers to new worlds.

2. In and Out Scene-Building: Keep things moving.

3. A Sole Dramatic Question: Build your foundation with a single brick.

4. Create Tension with the Three C's: The Clock: Place your action in the shadow of a ticking clock; The Crucible: Constrain your characters as you apply the heat; and The Contract: Make promises to your reader, and then keep them.

5. Specifics: Learn before you teach. Research, research, research.

6. Information Weaving: Dole out description in bite-sized chunks.

7. Revision: The most fun of all. After writing the first draft, go back and play with it.

As he began to research his third novel, *Deception Point*, Brown once again turned to the Internet. But this time, he looked to develop relationships with a couple of experts he could correspond with on a regular basis.

He continued to be surprised at the sheer volume of supposedly secret information readily available to anyone—online or off—who just started digging for it.

Since *Deception Point* revolved around the secret goings-on at NASA and other government agencies, Brown liberally relied on the Freedom of Information Act. "It's a great resource, primarily because it can lead to specific individuals who are knowledgeable in a given field and sometimes are willing to talk about it," he said. "In many cases, understandably, these contacts prefer to remain nameless, but sometimes, depending on what they've told you, they like being acknowledged in the book."

Like his two earlier novels, *Deception Point* would revolve around a secret society: NASA. And like the Vatican, the featured organization in *Angels & Demons*, NASA is one of the most covert secret societies in the world, while also one of the most public.

"For me, writing about clandestine material keeps me engaged in the project," he said. "Because a novel can take upwards of a year to write, I need to be constantly learning as I write, or I lose interest. Researching and writing about secretive topics helps remind me how fun it is to 'spy' into unseen worlds, and it motivates me to try to give the reader that same experience." Also as before, once a teacher, always a teacher. "My goal is always to make the characters and plot so engaging that readers don't realize how much they are learning along the way," he said.

■ ■ ■

Once Brown sent the manuscript for *Deception Point* to Kaufman, he and Blythe began to talk about the possibilities for his next novel, his fourth. It almost seemed like he was stuck in an endless loop of the movie *Groundhog Day*, for even though he continued to vow that he would never write another novel without a firm commitment from a publisher, once *Deception Point* was finished, he was essentially working without a net, since his third novel had satisfied his two-book contract with Simon & Schuster.

Deception Point wouldn't be published for at least another year, and the early sales figures for *Angels & Demons* were looking less than stellar. Brown took this opportunity to look for a new agent. There are many reasons why a writer in Brown's position would look for new representation. Publishing can be such a game of chance that sometimes a writer will believe that if he alters just one part of the equation—by switching publishers, agents, or even genres—the next book will sell significantly better than the previous one. Of course there are no guarantees, but many writers who consider a change feel that doing something, anything, is better than leaving things the way they are. So Brown fired his first agent, Jake Elwell, and signed on with

Dan Brown produced and wrote all the songs on *SynthAnimals*, which he released in 1989. (Courtesy of Ron Wallace)

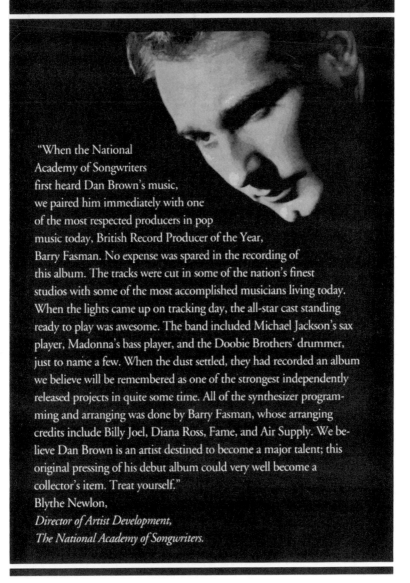

DAN BROWN

"When the National
Academy of Songwriters
first heard Dan Brown's music,
we paired him immediately with one
of the most respected producers in pop
music today, British Record Producer of the Year,
Barry Fasman. No expense was spared in the recording of
this album. The tracks were cut in some of the nation's finest
studios with some of the most accomplished musicians living today.
When the lights came up on tracking day, the all-star cast standing
ready to play was awesome. The band included Michael Jackson's sax
player, Madonna's bass player, and the Doobie Brothers' drummer,
just to name a few. When the dust settled, they had recorded an album
we believe will be remembered as one of the strongest independently
released projects in quite some time. All of the synthesizer program-
ming and arranging was done by Barry Fasman, whose arranging
credits include Billy Joel, Diana Ross, Fame, and Air Supply. We believe Dan Brown is an artist destined to become a major talent; this
original pressing of his debut album could very well become a
collector's item. Treat yourself."
Blythe Newlon,
Director of Artist Development,
The National Academy of Songwriters.

A three-page article on the *Dan Brown* CD appeared in *AfterTouch*. It was
written by Ron Wallace, owner of Creative Musicians Coalition. (Courtesy
of Ron Wallace)

The *Angels & Demons* CD was released in 1995. (Courtesy of Ron Wallace)

Brown, near his New Hampshire home, July 1998. (Photo: Greg Mironchuk/ PictureDesk International)

Brown in Exeter, New Hampshire, July 1998. (Photo: Greg Mironchuk/ PictureDesk International)

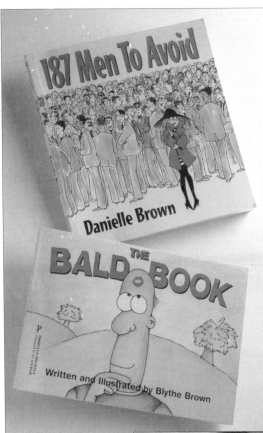

Dan Brown's first book, *187 Men to Avoid*, was published in 1995 under the pseudonym Danielle Brown. The copyright, however, is held by Dan Brown. *The Bald Book* was published in 1998. Although the byline reads "Written and illustrated by Blythe Brown," Dan Brown wrote it, according to Jake Elwell, the literary agent who represented the book.

Brown wearing the headset he used to dictate his novels to a computer via voice recognition software. (Photo: Greg Mironchuk/ PictureDesk International)

Bodyguards protect Brown from a cluster of photographers as he arrives in court, February 27, 2006. (Photo: Ben Graville/Rex USA)

Richard Leigh and Michael Baigent, authors of *Holy Blood, Holy Grail*, plaintiffs in the copyright infringement case against Random House. (Photo: Keith Waldegrave/*Mail on Sunday*/Rex/Rex USA)

Dan at the High Court in London, in the copyright infringement case against his publisher, March 9, 2006. (Photo: Paul Grover/Rex USA)

A visibly relieved Brown relaxes after the conclusion of the trial, March 14, 2006. (Photo: Eddie Mulholland/Rex USA)

Brown with actress Audrey Tautou, on a promotional Eurostar train trip from London to Cannes, May 16, 2006. (Photo: Scott Myers/Rex USA)

Dan and Blythe Brown at the premiere of *The Da Vinci Code* movie, at the 59th Cannes Film Festival in France, May 17, 2006. (Photo: Scott Myers/Rex USA)

Brown at the film premiere of *Angels and Demons* in Rome, May 4, 2009, with one of the Swiss Guards. (Photo: AGF s.r.l./Rex USA)

Dan Brown with Ron Howard and Tom Hanks at the film premiere of *Angels and Demons* in Rome, May 4, 2009. (Photo: AGF s.r.l./Rex USA)

Heide Lange of Sanford J. Greenburger Associates, a mid-sized agency in New York that represents authors of both serious and commercial fiction and nonfiction. The agency was founded in 1932 by its namesake and is well-known for its representation of European authors like Umberto Eco, Vaclav Havel, and the estate of Franz Kafka.

Dan, Blythe, and Heide knew that Dan's next novel had to absolutely knock everyone's socks off, or he may have to start using a pseudonym, as many novelists with mediocre sales on two or three novels had started to do.

Before deciding on the topic of his next book, they took a critical look at his previous novels to examine what worked and what didn't, as well as the sales figures for each, both of which were mediocre. *Angels & Demons* came out on top in the sales department. *Digital Fortress* had earned a significant amount of attention from the media, but they knew that part of its success stemmed from being a hot topic at the right time. It was impossible to determine how *Deception Point* would fare once it was released. But to Dan and Blythe, placing another novel in the Arctic was pretty much a non-issue.

Travel was their passion. The couple decided that any future books would be set either in warm-weather venues, so they could escape the bone-chilling winters of New Hampshire for research, or in cities with great museums and art opportunities—or in the best of both worlds, both.

"*Deception Point* was set in the Arctic Circle, and I learned very quickly that that was a bad idea," Brown joked. "I set *The Da Vinci Code* in Paris and London, and the three trips to Europe were all tax-deductible. You can go broke saving money on your taxes, but we had an absolutely wonderful time."

Brown knew that the novel would lead the characters on a treasure hunt in some fashion, and would place them in situations that were so dire it would seem impossible that anyone would be able to escape alive.

As the threesome continued their analysis, they determined that there were two more reasons *Digital Fortress* got so much media attention. First, the story featured a topic that most people dealt with in their daily lives but knew little about. Second, the novel revealed a secret the general public was shocked to discover. They brainstormed to think of a story line that could incorporate these two factors.

They were getting closer. Brown examined all the information that he had left out of *Angels & Demons* due to lack of space or the simple fact that he just couldn't find a place for it. After all, he had amassed so many interesting details in the course of doing the research for *Angels & Demons* that he couldn't have possibly squeezed it all into one book. This was perfectly understandable, given that the Catholic Church had centuries of history behind it while the history of both NASA and the NSA could be counted in mere decades.

He also thought about the aspects of his earlier novels that had offended people the most, or at least those that had spurred them to write to him. What could he dig up from his research that would generate instant publicity simply because it offended a particular group of people—the larger the better? He remembered that, after *Angels & Demons* was published, he got a lot of grief for describing the face on Bernini's statue of St. Teresa as looking like she was in the midst of a "toe-curling orgasm."

Sex combined with religion in any form was always a safe bet for generating controversy. So he decided that this would be part of the formula. It was at that point when he flashed back to the art history class he had taken at the University of Seville, in which the professor told the class that Leonardo Da Vinci's painting *The Last Supper* was filled with revealing secrets, particularly about the relationship between Jesus and Mary Magdalene.

And just like that, he had the hook on which he would hang the entire novel.

As the story line for the novel began to take shape in his

mind, the next decision to be made concerned the main characters. Should Brown create another protagonist from scratch or use one that had already played a starring role in his previous novels? Dan and Blythe were both partial to Robert Langdon. Of the three male protagonists in his novels, Robert Langdon had the most potential for multiple story lines, as his job and area of specialty could take him anywhere in the world. Plus, it was Robert Langdon who most closely resembled Brown's personality.

Indeed, Brown himself has admitted as much. "Langdon is the man I wish I were," he said. "Langdon is significantly cooler than I am. One of the luxuries of being a writer is that you can live vicariously through your characters.

"Langdon is a character who has my own interests," he said. "I am fascinated with ancient mysteries, art history, and codes. You spend a year, a year and a half, writing a book, you better be darn sure your hero is involved in the subject matter you are excited about."

Heide Lange agreed. "I think he embodies Robert Langdon," she said. "He is as smart as the character he has created. He is very engaging and playful. He is mentally invigorating."

Researching and writing a book that revolved around the secret codes that Leonardo da Vinci embedded in his art was a natural fit as well. After all, Brown strongly identified with the artist, the original Renaissance man. Leonardo da Vinci (1452–1519) was born in Italy and was an active participant in many different disciplines, from music, art, and anatomy to architecture and engineering. He was also an enthusiastic inventor of new technologies, many of which were realized centuries after his death. He loved to disassemble objects to see how they worked, and his interest naturally extended to human bodies.

It's easy to imagine Brown describing himself when talking about Da Vinci's motivations behind the codes and puzzles he devised. "There are many people who feel he did it partly to keep himself amused, and he was a prankster and he loved codes," he said. "He was fascinated with secrets and devised many ways to keep information secret and portray it in ways that most people, when they look at a painting, don't really see."

And perhaps Brown was also referring to himself with this statement: "Da Vinci was skilled enough as a painter, that if he had meant there to be some sort of androgynous controversy there, he certainly would have had the skills to avoid that, had he not wanted it there."

Most intriguing, perhaps, Brown felt the two saw eye to eye when it came to religion. "Surprisingly, despite Leonardo's long conflict with religion, he was a deeply spiritual man," he said. "His life's quest was to concoct a formula for everlasting life, and the Church considered this to be a heretical desire to cheat God of the final word. I think we have to assume that Leonardo failed in his quest to find a formula for everlasting life, but it was an interesting quest nonetheless." Soon enough, Brown would find himself on the receiving end of the kind of ecclesiastical reproach that was sometimes directed at Leonardo.

■ ■ ■

Once he had settled on using Robert Langdon as the protagonist with the secrets embedded in Leonardo da Vinci's art as the cornerstone for this make-or-break book, Brown got busy. In fact, it didn't take him long to decide that Robert Langdon would not only make a repeat performance in the next book but, assuming it was a success, in any novel he would write in the future.

So he decided to take a long-term approach and sketch out story lines for future books in the series that would feature Langdon. Brown saw this foresight as an excuse to indulge his love of codes and puzzles, and decided to plant clues about future novels featuring the symbologist in his fourth novel. Not only would this satisfy Brown's need to construct elaborate, brainy treasure hunts that took circuitous paths through all of his novels to come, but it would help hook readers on Langdon's future adventures and hopefully encourage strong sales, which would make him more valuable in the eye of whatever publisher he ended up with next.

In fact, Brown became so enamored with the idea of Robert Langdon as the star of what was turning (if only in his mind) into a series, that he proceeded to develop story lines and rough outlines for twelve future novels featuring the cryptologist, though he admitted, "Chances are I don't get to write them all."

Though some people might assume Brown was referring to a terminal illness that was preventing him from writing all twelve novels, it's more likely he was starting to get a better grasp on the entire process of writing a book similar in tone and content to *The Da Vinci Code*. He may have originally thought he could write a novel in two years or less—after all, from the time he started writing *Digital Fortress* in the spring of 1995 to the point where he handed in his manuscript for *The Da Vinci Code* in the spring of 2002 he averaged the research and writing of four novels in just about seven years. So from beginning his research to completing the writing, at the time he would have thought that he could definitely complete all twelve Langdon novels.

However, he would not have been able to predict that life would intrude to the extent that after his fourth thriller, his next book would take six long years to appear on the shelves.

Once all the pieces were in place, Brown started to dig through the research that was left over from *Angels & Demons*, and seek out new sources. His fourth novel would be a culmination of every interest and influence he'd ever had in his life: religion, codes, art, and secret societies. He knew it would be quite a feat to pull off.

And Dan Brown knew that, if he couldn't pull it off, it would be time to switch gears, *again*. He had no choice but to go for broke. Compared to the music business, he much preferred writing novels. Writing books was much more personal and time-consuming than music, and it involved almost no collaboration with people who thought they knew what was best for him. He didn't have to change his essence to fit the demands of the marketplace. If anything, he was encouraged to draw on his intellectual curiosity whenever possible. After all, publishing was filled with brainy, literate people just like him who wanted to learn something new with every book they write.

Brown felt right at home. He began to dream of what success would mean; he was already becoming a bit too familiar with what failure felt like.

CHAPTER SIX

LAST CHANCE

DECEPTION POINT, **BROWN'S** third novel, was published in August 2001, and things got off to a rocky start. He began to have doubts about the wisdom of proceeding with the research for his fourth novel, because his dream of becoming a full-time novelist appeared to dim.

As they did before, Dan and Blythe worked together to promote the book, but there was little to hang it on. While *Digital Fortress* easily gained media attention due to the timeliness of online security issues, and *Angels & Demons* could be marketed through its travel-guide angle, it was a bit of a stretch to find a viable hook for *Deception Point,* a story that involved a glacier, NASA, and a power-hungry president.

And then the events of September 11, 2001, stopped everything in its tracks. Promising books of fiction and nonfiction published that fall went nowhere—*Deception Point* among them—and many details of the typical thriller novel suddenly seemed too frivolous. In addition, the presidential corruption angle in Brown's third novel was no longer viable in a new environment of patriotism and bipartisanship. The only information most Americans wanted to hear was how to distinguish anthrax from other white powdery substances and the best way to secure sheets of clear plastic to windows with duct tape.

For Dan Brown, September 11, 2001, began like any other. He was sequestered in his no-tech office in downtown Exeter, slogging away on *The Da Vinci Code*, when, quite unexpectedly, Blythe walked in to tell him the news.

His first response, based on the research he had conducted for *Digital Fortress*, said it all. "I instantly knew that it had finally happened," he said, referring to the one terrorist attack that had slipped through the cracks. He spent the next couple of months unable to work. "Writing fiction felt totally unimportant," he said. "With so much going on in the world, how can you afford to allow yourself the luxury of moving fictional characters around in a fictional landscape? How are you helping your country doing that?" He ultimately decided that, by going forward with his work on *The Da Vinci Code*, he was indeed helping his country. "I was giving people release from the pain of reality and some recreation," he said. "It's just hard to remember that."

Perhaps it was world events, or because *The Da Vinci Code* was Brown's most ambitious novel by far, but he and Blythe began to work more closely together than they had on his previous books—*much* more closely. Her expertise in the primary subject of the book—the art of Leonardo Da Vinci—played an important role.

"My wife is an enormous influence," said Brown. "Her knowledge and her passion for the subject matter certainly buoys the process when it bogs down." And with the intricate story line and tight plotting of *The Da Vinci Code*, he bogged down more often than he would have liked. "Writing a book is incredibly hard. I would not wish it on my worst enemy," he said.

"There are days when it helps to have somebody around— especially in the case of *The Da Vinci Code*—who understands art and Da Vinci and is passionate about it and can say, 'Let's go take a walk and talk about why we got into this in the first place, what's so exciting about Da Vinci and what he believed,'" he said. "I'm very fortunate on that front."

■ ■ ■

The time Brown spent working on *The Da Vinci Code* changed more than just his relationship with his wife. His views toward religion and spirituality began to shift as he delved more deeply into his research. It didn't take long for cracks to appear in the foundation.

"You can't research this explosive a topic and become so immersed in this kind of subject matter without having your fundamental philosophy altered," he said. "I began the research for *The Da Vinci Code* as a skeptic. I entirely expected, as I researched the book, to disprove this theory. After numerous trips to Europe, and about two years of research, I really became a believer. And it's important to remember that this is a novel about a theory that has been out there for a long time."

The facts he was uncovering did not match what he had been taught as a child, both in school and at church. "I was troubled by these differences, so I asked an historian friend of mine, 'How do historians balance contrary accounts of the same event?' And he responded in what I thought was a brilliant way," he said. "He told me that when we read and interpret history, we are not interpreting the historical events themselves. We are interpreting written accounts of those events. In essence, we are interpreting people's interpretations.

"Many historians now believe that in engaging the historical accuracy of concepts, we should first ask ourselves a far deeper question: How historically accurate is history itself? In most cases we will never know the answer. But that should not stop us from asking the questions."

With that simple concept, a new lightbulb went on for Brown.

He began to suspect that this book would turn out to be very different from his first three, despite featuring the protagonist from *Angels & Demons*. "I think as I was writing I knew there was something special about it," he said. Whether it was the controversial subject matter, the opportunity to probe

Robert Langdon's character more deeply, or the simple fact that he had absolutely nothing to lose and, therefore, poured his entire soul into writing the story, Brown had a sense that his fourth novel would be unique.

Jack Heath's words—*Simpler is better*—echoed in his ears, but Brown still hadn't mastered the art of tight writing in his first few drafts. He had to spill everything onto the page first and then go back and cut out up to 90 percent of what he had written.

"Writing an informative yet compact thriller is a lot like making maple sugar candy," he said. "You have to tap hundreds of trees, boil vats and vats of raw sap, evaporate the water, and keep boiling until you've distilled a tiny nugget that encapsulates the essence.

"I very liberally used my delete key," he explained. "For every single page in *The Da Vinci Code* that a reader reads, there are ten pages that ended up in the trash can. This is above all a thriller. And I tried to use just that information that really served the story and helped move the plot along."

But the work on his fourth novel presented an even greater challenge for him, due not only to its subject matter, but also the sheer amount of information and obscure facts he wanted to cram into the text. He had to research many different aspects of all the data he intended to weave into the narrative, not just the history of the various works of art and the locations of each scene in the novel.

"I worked very hard to make all of this sort of arcane information accessible and exciting," he said. "A symbologist, as the name implies, is somebody who understands symbols. For example, he's somebody who might be able to look at the eye inside the triangle on the back of the dollar bill. He might be able to know where that came from, what it means, its historical significance."

He noted that one trip he and Blythe took to Europe was particularly special. "We were given access to all sorts of areas in the Louvre that normally we would not have been given access to," he said, which included sections of the museum that he didn't even know existed. "There are restoration labs there that look like NASA clean rooms, and a security facility that looks like Fort Knox."

Brown estimated that the couple's visit to the non-public sections of the Louvre required months of planning and networking. But even in his pre-*Da Vinci Code* days, Dan had a number of strings he could pull to gain access to secret files and areas. "After writing three books about secret societies, I've made a lot of friends in those secret circles," he said, adding that he was continually surprised by how eager people are to talk to him for a book about something they love. "Most people are dying to tell me what they know. And I have always been very grateful for that," he said.

"A lot of people tell me the Internet must be really helpful, but you know, it really isn't, because so much of what is on the Internet is not accurate and is silly," he said. "It's almost harder to sort through the amount of strangeness to find the actual true bits on the Internet. It's much easier to go to Paris and track down some people at the Louvre who know a lot about Da Vinci and talk to them, or read books by reputable historians." Brown noted that he still conducted the bulk of his research by reading books. "I had so many requests for my bibliography that I finally just posted it on my Web site," he said. Once again he turned to the services of Stan Planton, the Ohio University research librarian, who had proved to be so helpful in digging up obscure facts for his second and third novels.

From the start, Brown viewed *The Da Vinci Code* as a way to educate the reader about the intricacies and history of the Priory of Sion and Opus Dei and introduce people to the hidden codes in the art of Leonardo da Vinci. And so, while he used his own extensive library of books on art history and religion, as well as a band of researchers who specialized in esoteric facets of these subjects, he knew Planton could help him in ways that no one else could. As before, the librarian conducted the research for the novelist free of charge.

"On reflection, that might not have been a good career move, but I was helping an unknown author who had what I considered great potential," said Planton. "The thought of a contractual relationship never entered my mind."

When it came to including the theory that Jesus and Mary Magdalene were husband and wife, again, Brown started out a skeptic. By the end, however, he had turned around. While he may have been hesitant to explore the topic, he soon came to believe that given the current state of religion and spirituality in America today, readers might be more receptive to the theory than he had assumed. "I really got the sense that people were ready for this story," he said. "It was the type of thing that people were ready to hear."

In the end, "*The Da Vinci Code* describes history as I have come to understand it through many years of travel, research, reading, interviews, and exploration," he said.

From the beginning, Blythe served as the inspiration for *The Da Vinci Code*. For one, Dan dedicated the book to her. "My wife, Blythe, was an enormous help in the research of this novel, and possibly, just possibly, had something to do with the recurring theme of the goddess and the sacred feminine," he said. "She is an enormous Da Vinci fanatic and really got me extremely interested in this topic. I became a believer the more time we spent in Europe in these museums. Plus, she's a great editor."

However, despite the tightly formatted plotting and intriguing and controversial story line, at the end of 2001, there was some chance that *The Da Vinci Code* might not ever see the light of day. The sales figures for *Deception Point* were downright abysmal. The only comfort they could take was that they weren't alone: The 2001 terrorist attacks and changes in the structure of book retailing had plunged the entire book publishing industry into a crippling economic depression—and this was especially true for thrillers.

The decreased sales generally, and Brown's mediocre sales record for his three novels in particular, did not bode well for the novel he was currently pouring his soul—and days—into. Through most of the history of modern book publishing, editors and publishers understood it took time for readers to discover a book series that featured a continuing protagonist. A reader would typically start by reading the most recently published book by an author, and if he liked it, in time he would work his way back and purchase all the earlier novels, sometimes making a publisher's backlist—those titles published at least a year before—more profitable than the book that was most recently released.

At least that's the way things used to work, in the days when most publishers were independently owned and could afford the luxury of allowing an unknown author to build a following over the course of five or more books. In some cases, this could take a decade or more. Beginning in the 1990s, international corporations saw money and prestige in book publishing companies—especially if they could tie them into other media outlets they owned to facilitate cross-promotion—and so they began snapping up privately owned publishers by the cartload.

And they needed to make a profit. While publishers of old were primarily interested in producing good literature, the first concern of the conglomerates was financial. Whether a successful book had a literary bent or was more commercial in flavor didn't matter. Making a profit and pleasing the stockholders did. This meant if an author's first couple of books didn't immediately begin to draw an audience that would be hungry for more, there was no reason to offer another contract. In some cases, a publisher might even pay the balance of a multibook advance to an author but never actually publish the remaining books. For an author with a sales history similar to Dan Brown's first three books, this would be the quickest way for a publisher to cut its losses.

"I'm glad I'm not beginning now," said veteran author Dean Koontz, whose books now sell approximately seventeen million copies each year. "When I started out, you had years to find a voice. In the old days, bookstores bought on hope. Now, if a new writer has a book and it sells to a specific level, the second book is expected to show a significant increase. He might get a third chance, and then he becomes anathema. Publishers want hits fast and they want bigger successes. They aren't as interested in building writers, and that's the tragedy of publishing today. I know a lot of writers who needed a lot of books before they finally found their voice."

Worse yet, the publication of Dan Brown's first three novels coincided with the phenomenal growth and public acceptance of e-commerce, including the sale of used books by both mom-and-pop outfits and offshoots of the largest bookstore chains. One copy of a book might be sold several times over the course of its life, but the only time its sale would earn money for its publisher—and royalties for its author—would be in the original sale as a new book.

There was more bad news. Brown's editor at Simon & Schuster was actively job-hunting again. Although Jason Kaufman had become Brown's editor by default, he had handled both *Angels & Demons* and *Deception Point*, and both author and editor had developed a comfortable working relationship.

Fortunately, Kaufman had a real hunch about Dan Brown, and about the new book, and he decided that accepting his next editorial position would be contingent on whether he could bring Brown on board with him.

When Kaufman interviewed at Doubleday and president Stephen Rubin heard about Kaufman's conditions of employment, he balked. But despite the stranglehold that the conglomerates have on book publishing, there are still gutsy editors and publishers around who are willing to take a chance on authors who haven't broken away from the pack. It helped that Brown had a two-hundred-page outline of his fourth novel all ready to go.

"The first thing Jason did when he came here was say, 'I want to bring in a writer named Dan Brown.' We said, 'Who's

Dan Brown?' He had a proposal for a new book, which turned out to be *The Da Vinci Code*," said Stephen Rubin.

Rubin read the proposal and liked what he saw. He then read *Angels & Demons* to get an idea of how Brown handled the first book that featured Robert Langdon and how the author was able to incorporate arcane facts into a fast-moving plot. Other editors read it and, like Rubin, they liked what they saw. Doubleday made an offer.

Kaufman got the job, Brown got a two-book contract worth $400,000 that Heide Lange negotiated, and Doubleday got a new author and a new editor. In retrospect, it was a gutsy move on Kaufman's part. "But I thought if a guy like Dan couldn't bring it all together, then who could?"

The truth is that Jason Kaufman's move to Doubleday was probably the best thing that could have happened at that point in Dan Brown's career. If he had stayed at Simon & Schuster— assuming the publisher would have offered a new contract, which was doubtful given the sales figures of the author's two novels with the house—*The Da Vinci Code* would have launched with little fanfare. The publicity department would have printed and distributed perhaps 250 advanced reading copies, and the first printing would have been five thousand to ten thousand copies. Dan and Blythe would have done their usual publicity dog-and-pony show, and the book would have followed the path of his previous novels.

Given Brown's track record with Pocket Books, especially since he no longer had an editor at the house willing to go to bat for him with the other departments, the publisher was probably happy to let Kaufman take Dan Brown with him when he left.

■ ■ ■

Once Jason Kaufman had officially joined Doubleday, Brown could turn his full attention to researching and writing *The Da Vinci Code*. He also worked harder than before to continue the pattern he set with his earlier novels and place codes in the text.

Since he already had a dozen rough outlines for future novels featuring Robert Langdon, Brown decided to place clues that would come into play in later books down the road. However, unlike the first three books, where the codes and puzzles were largely unbeknownst to most readers caught up in reading a fast-moving, tightly plotted novel, in *The Da Vinci Code* he would switch gears and deliberately make them part of the story line. If readers deciphered the code before one of the characters figured it out, that was fine. However, he also made sure that each code was solved and explained in the text before proceeding to the next.

For once, it looked like Dan Brown's fortunes were improving. He had a new publisher, a new book deal, and a contract that paid an advance that virtually obligated the publisher to commit big money and make a real effort to promote his new novel.

He was finally on his way.

CHAPTER SEVEN

CHANGING **FORTUNES**

IN LATE 2002, publication of *The Da Vinci Code* was still a few months away, but the wheels had been turning for months. For once, Dan and Blythe were pleasantly surprised.

"A few months before the book came out, I started hearing from booksellers who had read advance copies," he said. "They were so unbelievably enthusiastic that I started to suspect that the book would do well."

Perhaps because of the size of his advance from Doubleday and because of the buzz that was building over the book by booksellers, the art department broke with tradition and listened to Brown's suggestions for the front and back covers of his fourth novel, as well as the inside flaps. Brown had suggested placing codes and clues about the story right on the cover to make the entire book a total package. While Da Vinci's *Last Supper* featured more prominently in the plot of the novel, a reproduction of the *Mona Lisa* was ultimately chosen to appear on the cover, probably because it is more universally recognized than *The Last Supper*.

Brown also provided ideas about the design of the copy that appeared on the inside book flap of the dustjacket. To most readers, the codes would go unnoticed, but Doubleday hoped they would help build intrigue among readers. "We had to find a way to get velocity on Day One," said Rubin.

Late in 2002 Doubleday printed ten thousand galleys—or advanced reading copies—to distribute to booksellers, book reviewers, and others in the trade. That number alone was larger than the number of copies in the first printings of any of Brown's first three novels.

Once the galleys were in circulation, the response and feedback from early readers was immediate and positive. Based on the advance orders that booksellers were placing for the book, Doubleday scheduled a first printing of 230,000 copies of *The Da Vinci Code* for publication on March 18, 2003.

Another good signal for the book's success was that Brown began conducting interviews with the media well in advance of the publication date, so reporters and editors could have the story all ready to go once the book was officially out. And for the first time, the publisher's publicity department took full responsibility for media interviews and contacts, which meant that Blythe could relax.

The day before the official launch of Brown's fourth novel, cartons of books waited in stockrooms, ready to be unboxed and shelved by bookstore staffers the following day.

Then the planets aligned.

While book review media aimed at booksellers and others in the industry tend to print their reviews months before a book's scheduled publication date to facilitate ordering by bookstores, newspaper book review sections operate on a different schedule. Unless it's a big-name author or a favorite local writer, book reviews in magazines and newspapers often don't appear until a month or two after a book first arrives on bookstore shelves. Since the average shelf life for most new books is ninety days or less before it gets shipped back to the distributor, these delays in publishing reviews have caused many an author—of both fiction and nonfiction—to complain about the lack of sales and visibility for their titles in bookstores.

On St. Patrick's Day 2003, the day before the official publication date for *The Da Vinci Code*, the *New York Times* broke all the rules by printing book critic Janet Maslin's glowing review of

The Da Vinci Code. The review included the following accolades:

> *The word is wow.*
>
> *In this gleefully erudite suspense novel, Brown takes the format he has been developing through three earlier novels and fine-tunes it to blockbuster perfection.*
>
> *The book moves at a breakneck pace, with the author seeming thoroughly to enjoy his contrivances.*
>
> *Virtually every chapter ends with a cliffhanger: not easy, considering the amount of plain old talking that gets done.*

Probably one of the most important things that Maslin did in her review was to compare Brown's fourth novel to the Harry Potter novels by J. K. Rowling. While Brown admitted that at that point he hadn't yet read any of the Harry Potter novels, he said he was dumbfounded at Maslin's review. "People called and said, 'Is Janet Maslin your mother, because she never says stuff like that,'" he said.

Perhaps it was the teacher in him that zeroed in on the Harry Potter connection, since he would later point to how children reacted to his book as one of the most satisfying—and surprising results. "Kids have really reacted—especially to *The Da Vinci Code* and *Angels & Demons,*" he said. "It's like a more mature Harry Potter, I guess, is what a lot of kids are feeling. It has some of those ancient mystery elements that people like in Harry Potter."

"We were out of our minds on Day One," said Doubleday's president, Stephen Rubin. "We had a terrific ad campaign, a hot-house review on the front of the *Times* arts section, and in-your-face distribution in bookstores across the country.

"The stores had taken such an outlandish number of books that they knew they couldn't depend on the publisher alone, so they did a tremendous amount of work on their side. I've never seen a sales force and bookselling community take ownership of a book like they did with *The Da Vinci Code*."

Everyone had high hopes for the book, thinking perhaps it had a shot of hitting the *New York Times* best-seller list for a couple of weeks, but no one could have expected the runaway success and the public appetite for Everything Dan Brown that would gradually gain momentum and then absolutely snowball.

"We always acknowledged that we had something exceptional, but I don't think any of us knew how extraordinary it was," said Rubin. "It's a thriller for people who don't like thrillers. It's tremendously engaging as a reading experience, while at the same time, you are learning something."

Its first day on sale, *The Da Vinci Code* sold 6,000 copies, jumping to almost 24,000 by the end of the first week. The following week, the first issues of the best-seller lists for *Publishers Weekly*, the *Wall Street Journal*, and Barnes & Noble covering the first day that *The Da Vinci Code* was in the stores hit. Dan Brown was three thousand miles from home, in the middle of a book tour, heading from one media interview to another, when he got the news that *The Da Vinci Code* was on them.

"He heard the news when he was in Seattle," said Blythe. "He had no friends, no family with him. He was just walking the streets of Seattle."

The book hit the top of the *New York Times* best-seller list for hardcover fiction a few days later.

Finally, after slogging away at his dream for eight long years, he had made it. If there was one thing his experience doing publicity for his first three novels had taught him, it was how to talk with reporters. He knew what they wanted. While offering up intriguing sound bites and quotes, he took meticulous care not to reveal any of the surprises in the novel.

He did express surprise at the instant popularity of the book, however, and tried to explain it by putting several different spins on things.

"I would love to say it's about the writing and it's about the storytelling, and it is a fun read, but I think the real reason has more to do with the subject matter," he said. "The book incorporates Leonardo da Vinci's artwork, which everyone loves; codes; and most of all, secrets—ancient historical secrets which interest us all. But the book makes you consider history in new ways and your own spirituality in new ways. [It] makes you look at things you thought you understood and suddenly see them differently."

With *The Da Vinci Code*, Dan Brown had gone from representing a significant investment for Doubleday to being one of the publisher's cash cows, at least for the time being. As her client's reputation and value had literally changed overnight, Brown's agent went into overdrive to maximize his value to the publisher. Lange had originally sold *The Da Vinci Code* as the first book in a two-book contract for an advance of $400,000.

Once it became clear that *The Da Vinci Code* was not just any novel, in terms of the money it was generating for the publisher, Lange renegotiated his contract with Doubleday. After all, Brown had more than made his advance back for *The Da Vinci Code* when the first printing of 230,000 copies of the novel sold out. She secured a longer multibook contract with the publisher, increasing the number of novels Brown was obligated to write for Doubleday—featuring Robert Langdon and no one else—from two books to four.

Of course, the original contract was a legally binding document and Doubleday technically could have just honored its terms and then held out for a brand-new contract after Brown handed in the manuscript for *The Lost Symbol*. But by then the feeding frenzy among other publishers would have been something to witness, and Doubleday wanted to make sure its new golden goose didn't jump the fence.

Dan Brown was more than on his way. He was the bestselling author in the United States. "Dan Brown" had just become a franchise.

CHAPTER EIGHT

RUNAWAY SUCCESS

BROWN WAS STUNNED by the attention generated by the publication of *The Da Vinci Code*. And that attention was occurring not only in the United States and at the Vatican, but all over the world as well.

"It's entirely shocking," he told Matt Lauer during an appearance on the *Today* show.

Ten weeks after *The Da Vinci Code* was published, there were a million copies in print in the United States. Doubleday president Stephen Rubin would later comment that the only book that sold in comparable numbers—and with a similar frenzy in its first year of publication—was *The Bridges of Madison County* by Robert James Waller, which was published in 1992 and sold six million copies in two years. *The Da Vinci Code*, of course, would have Waller's book handily beat; by the time Brown's book had been in print for one year, it had sold 6.5 million copies in the United States alone, a figure that ballooned to more than ten million copies at the end of two years.

But that was only the beginning. What happened next—not only to sales of *The Da Vinci Code* but to all of Brown's earlier novels—had never happened in the history of book publishing.

Brown's fourth novel struck such a chord in readers that after they devoured *The Da Vinci Code*—sometimes reading the entire book, cover to cover, in one sitting—they were so enthralled they began to buy his previous three novels.

When orders suddenly began to come in to St. Martin's Press for *Digital Fortress* and to Simon & Schuster for *Angels & Demons* and *Deception Point*, the publishers were caught off guard. None of these titles had sold more than a handful of copies in the year before *The Da Vinci Code* came out. Once Brown's former publishers realized what was happening, they designed new covers—which of course featured the name *Dan Brown* in letters that were almost as large as the title—and ordered new printings. And then, even more shocking, one by one, each of these novels began to hit the best-seller lists all over the country. Occasionally, all four of his published novels appeared in the same week.

It was customary for a publisher to produce new editions of an author's earlier books if pay dirt is struck with a later book. But a five-year-old, obscure first novel like *Digital Fortress* making the lists? Impossible. It had never been done before.

The controversy about what Brown had affirmed was true in *The Da Vinci Code*—that Jesus and Mary Magdalene were husband and wife—intrigued many people enough to buy the book, but angered many more, whether or not they had actually read the book. Many of them—priests, lay Catholics, evangelical and other protestant Christians, even the Vatican—demanded equal time in the media to denounce Brown's theories and his book. Heightened curiosity about the book drove sales even higher. People clamored for more—anything written by Dan Brown. He had hit pay dirt. *Finally.*

In the wake of this increased visibility, Brown decided to tinker with the acknowledgments he had written for at least one of his previous novels. When *Angels & Demons* was published, he was still represented by Jake Elwell of Wieser and Wieser (which had since become Wieser and Elwell), and Brown had thanked his agent, whom he referred to as "my friend"; he had not yet met Heide Lange.

However, once *The Da Vinci Code* took off, Brown rewrote the acknowledgments in his second novel. After thanking his editor Jason Kaufman in the first paragraph, Brown wrote, "To the incomparable Heide Lange—to whom *Angels & Demons* guided me—for giving this novel new life at home and for bringing it to the world."

Elwell got shunted down to the fourth paragraph of kudos: "To my first agent, Jake Elwell, for his early help and for selling this novel to Pocket Books." Brown also dropped the words "my friend" that had appeared before Elwell's name in early editions of *Angels & Demons*.

■ ■ ■

Dan Brown's suggestion to place codes in the flap copy and on the cover itself paid off. In November 2003, ABC's *Good Morning America* held a contest for viewers to find all of the codes hidden in plain sight on the cover. Before the contest, Brown admitted being surprised at the lack of people who had noticed the hidden codes.

Perhaps Doubleday executives thought that sales of the book would start to drop off in November, so in order to maintain interest through the holiday season, they developed an online treasure hunt called the "Original Da Vinci Code Challenge" in cooperation with *Good Morning America*. Indeed, the contest was perfectly positioned to increase holiday sales, since the winner of the contest wouldn't be announced until two weeks into 2004.

Here's how it worked: Viewers would go online to the official contest Web site and decipher the clues. But they could submit their names only after they had solved all four codes. In essence, Brown had great fun watching viewers duplicate the Christmas morning treasure hunts of his childhood. In fact, one has to wonder if he was reluctant to appear on the show that announced the winner, since Brown essentially had to give away the answers to viewers who were too lazy to figure them out on their own. Perhaps it's no accident that after the contest was over, Brown placed a moratorium on future media interviews and talk-show appearances.

By the way, these four codes were only those he had publicly acknowledged. "There may be more," he said, cryptically as ever. "There are four codes visible to the naked eye on this jacket."

After suggesting that readers tilt the book in good light in order to notice one of the codes, he provided them with the first hint as he pointed to a blown-up copy of the cover. "Right here in the flap copy, in the phrase *while in Paris on business*, there's something different about the word *business* if you look closely at the word," he said.

Using a huge blown-up version of the cover and the flaps, Brown then guided viewers through the rest of the first code. "Follow down to the word *symbologist*," he said. "You'll find the letter S, and if you follow it, you get a phrase that is a distress call for a secret society."

Perhaps the way that acutely points to how he interprets historical facts and takes certain liberties was evident when he explained the first code on *Good Morning America*. After revealing that some of the letters in the dust jacket flaps had been "darkened," Brown went on to admit, "Technically this isn't really a code," he told host Charles Gibson. "This is just hidden language." The darkened letters spelled out "Is there no help for the widow's son," which is a distress call among Freemasons.

He then led the audience through the rest of the codes. A name was chosen from viewers who had been able to correctly identify all four codes—those that were visible to the naked eye, one assumes—and had sent in their answers. The winner received a trip for two to Paris and a personally designed list of secret locations in the city—Brown didn't say whether these sites were mentioned in the book, either in plain sight or in code.

Brown admitted that he was flabbergasted at the idea that forty thousand people had actually correctly deciphered all four codes, and that hundreds of thousands of others had tried but not finished.

■ ■ ■

Brown's rising tide began to lift other boats as well. As his fortunes grew, the Dan Brown Machine naturally brought others along.

As a result of his association with his star author, Jason Kaufman, Brown's editor, has been accorded superstar status among editors. However, like his most famous author, he prefers to keep a low profile. Before his personal stock rose in the publishing industry with the stellar success of *The Da Vinci Code*, Kaufman had a reputation of being a middle-of-the-road kind of editor, handling both fiction and nonfiction, but with no real breakout books. Some of his projects with previous publishers included books that ranged from golf to health and medical topics.

For Kaufman, it was a catch-22 situation: Since he didn't have the reputation for shepherding anything but middle-of-the-road projects from proposal through to finished books, literary agents only sent him these kinds of books. Not to mention the fact that, since his average tenure at his previous employers was less than two years, he often didn't get first look at top-shelf manuscripts and proposals.

After *Da Vinci*, of course, the tables have turned dramatically.

Today, Kaufman gets first look at many top-tier books and proposals that he would have never been offered before, since many agents now believe he has the golden touch. Some of these titles are little more than pale imitations of *The Da Vinci Code* or Brown's previous novels, and Kaufman rejects them all. "All these people who are looking for the next Dan Brown are going to be looking for a very long time," he said. In fact, in the year after *The Da Vinci Code* was published, he's only bought one work of fiction, although he does admit that when he does acquire a new book, the foreign publication rights tend to sell quickly and with greater frequency than before.

"Success has made me more cautious, because I want to find

something as fresh as *The Da Vinci Code*," he said. "I want to publish books that don't just do a genre really well, but push it in a new direction."

At the same time, Brown has made it clear that he won't go anywhere without Kaufman as his editor. While many publishers undoubtedly fantasize about the opportunity to whisk Brown away from Doubleday after his seventh novel is published—which will fulfill the fourth book in his revamped contract—it's clear that Brown and Kaufman work as a team. You want one, you get both—a deal publishers would happily embrace, but would undoubtedly have to pay dearly for.

In turn, Kaufman's role in Brown's life has taken on increased importance. This is especially true given that the publication of Brown's fifth novel was nowhere in sight as of late 2005. While Brown was previously capable of juggling work on a novel-in-progress while promoting another, it appears he's hit a major roadblock with this one. Before his name became a household word, Brown relied mostly on his wife and the delete key on his computer to whittle an unwieldy manuscript down to size.

But the totally unexpected response to *The Da Vinci Code* and the pressure to produce a novel that is just as entertaining, educating, and page turning have forced Brown to rely on Kaufman to an extent he hadn't previously. According to Kaufman, the two talked at least once a day about *The Lost Symbol*, and often more frequently than that.

"We go over every plot point and twist," says Kaufman. "I function as a sounding board for him."

Once Dan Brown turned into a bona fide celebrity, he began to limit his contact with the outside world. For one, he had to stop flying on commercial airlines because, once fellow passengers recognized him, he had no peace. They treated him like a rock star and would line up in the aisle so he could sign a copy of one of his books they just happened to bring on the flight. One imaginative passenger, lacking a copy of *The Da Vinci Code*, actually thrust an airsickness bag in front of the author to sign.

Brown was surprised by his sudden notoriety. "I have no idea how real celebrities handle their fame," he said. "I'm just a guy who wrote a book, and it still can turn into a circus at times when I go out in public. My life has changed dramatically."

As he continued to withdraw from the outside world, he began to reach out more to those who had known him in his pre–*Da Vinci Code* days. Librarian Stan Planton helped Brown puzzle out complicated information for *The Lost Symbol*. Brown has deepened his relationship with the librarian who has provided him with so much invaluable assistance through the years.

After a couple of earlier occasions where Brown and Planton were finally able to meet face-to-face, the author and his wife invited the librarian and his family to visit them on the seacoast, where they were guests in the Browns' home.

■ ■ ■

Signs that Brown would not be able to meet the deadline for his next book appeared very early on. He simply was too busy. "The positive response to *The Da Vinci Code* has changed my life dramatically," he said. "For one, here I am sitting on the *Today* show talking to Matt Lauer. That's a new experience. At the same time, I'm a writer. I spend my life essentially alone at a computer. That doesn't change. I have the same challenges every day."

As was his habit, Brown began research on his next novel long before the first copy of *The Da Vinci Code* rolled off the presses. But this time, the demand for his time and sound bites began to cut into his writing time.

"As far as my editors know, I'm working very hard on my next book," he joked about a month after *The Da Vinci Code* was published. In the wake of the stunning success of the book, he discovered what it was like to have a publisher go from viewing him as a risk and a liability to its most valuable asset. He had mixed feelings about it.

"I had assumed that I would have more control over the rate at which my books were delivered, when in fact I have less," he said. "The better my book does, the faster the publisher wants the next one. And of course, I am indebted to them because they have created this wonderful hit, but the irony is that I spend so much time on the radio and on the road that my writing schedule is interfered with."

At the same time, competent interviewers, picking up on the early clamor for everything Dan Brown, would have been remiss if they neglected to ask the author about his next novel. Stephen Rubin and the publicity team at Doubleday advised him to drop a few choice crumbs and leave it at that. And so he admitted that his fifth novel would be set in Washington, D.C., and that it would involve the Freemasons, but he stopped short of offering any more detail. "That's about all I'm allowed to say," he told one interviewer.

And then Brown began to get deluged with requests from other authors asking him to read their manuscripts and provide a glowing recommendation, or "blurb," for the back cover. Before *The Da Vinci Code* had been out for a month, he was receiving at least one manuscript or advanced reading copy each day. "I've never had so many friends in my life," he said. "If I read every manuscript that was sent to me, I'd never write another word."

Between the countless media interviews he was doing and trying to keep up with the research and writing on his next book, it didn't take long for him to fall behind.

■ ■ ■

As publishers from all over the world snapped up the rights to publish *The Da Vinci Code* in their jurisdictions—as of summer 2005, the book had been published in forty-four different languages—it didn't take long for Hollywood to come calling. Brown was initially reluctant, for more than a few reasons.

"Because Langdon is a series character, I'm hesitant to sell the film rights," he said. "One of the beauties of the reading experience is that everybody pictures Langdon in his or her perfect way. The second you slap a character in a script—no matter how you describe Langdon or any other character—they picture Ben Affleck or Hugh Jackman or whoever it happens to be."

And perhaps after living in Los Angeles for several years, Brown was all too familiar with the way people in the entertainment industry could view a project, especially a red-hot property that may mean significant profits from the first day of release.

"Hollywood has a way of taking a story like this and turning it into a car chase through Paris with machine guns and karate chops," he said. "So I'm very hesitant, but I'm talking to a few specific individuals who are the kinds of people who could make this a smart movie, and that's the only way I would sell, is if I had exceptional amounts of control."

And so, he continued to wait, although one director would eventually agree to Brown's every demand: Ron Howard. As it turned out, *The Da Vinci Code* movie would be released three years in the future, in the spring of May 2006, with Tom Hanks in the role of Robert Langdon.

■ ■ ■

As could be expected, it didn't take long for other authors to surface, accusing Brown of copying points they had made in earlier, more obscure books.

Three months after *The Da Vinci Code* was published, Doubleday received a letter from Lewis Perdue, an author of numerous nonfiction books and novels, who alleged that Dan Brown's fourth novel had plagiarized two of his previous novels: *The Da Vinci Legacy*, published in 1983, and *Daughter of God*, which came out in 2000. Perdue accused Brown of borrowing the themes and plots from his novels and liberally using them as the basis of the story for *The Da Vinci Code*.

Doubleday dismissed Perdue's complaint, as did Brown. But the publisher, perhaps sensing that Perdue would seek litigation in the future, beat him to the punch and filed suit in a federal court in Manhattan to request a declaratory judgment to the effect that *The Da Vinci Code* in no way infringed on the copyrights that Perdue holds for his two novels. In response, Perdue countersued for damages of $150 million, charging both Brown and Random House—the parent company of Doubleday—with copyright infringement. He also named Sony Pictures and Columbia Pictures as parties in the suit, since these film companies would co-produce the movie version of *The Da Vinci Code*.

While the cases made their way through the legal system before a pretrial hearing, Perdue got busy smearing Brown in the national and local media as well as through several Web sites—including davincicrock.blogspot.com and writopia.blogspot.com—where he uploaded the full-length depositions and other legal documents filed by both sides. Perdue also posted rebuttals and queries on public forums and bulletin boards at other Web sites that analyzed and discussed Brown's fourth novel.

Indeed, the questions Perdue publicly asked sounded like they could have appeared on the back of a best-selling thriller where one unknown-but-published novelist accuses a best-selling internationally famous novelist of plagiarizing his work:

1. Did Dan Brown and/or someone working with him plagiarize my work?
2. Why would Dan Brown not testify under oath that he didn't plagiarize me?
3. What role did Jason Kaufman play?
4. Who really did the research?
5. Who really wrote *The Da Vinci Code*?
6. Why has Blythe Brown sustained a strange alias,

Ahamedd Saaddoodeen, for more than twenty-
five years?
7. Why does Random House think their case is so
shaky that they have to misrepresent the truth?
8. Why can Random House *not* afford to allow this
to go to trial?

The only public comment Brown made on the topic at the
time was to essentially shrug off Perdue's accusations.

"Apparently this happens all the time to best-selling
authors," said Brown, revealing that, when *The Da Vinci Code*
debuted at number one, he received phone calls from several best-
selling authors, first to congratulate him, and then to warn him.
These seasoned best-selling authors said, "Well, get ready because
there are going to be people that you've never heard of coming out
of the woodwork who will want to ride on your coattails."

"All I can really say is I've never heard of Perdue and I've never
heard of his work," said Brown. "It's just one of those dubious badges
of honor that you wear once you hit the best-seller list, I guess."

In the spring of 2005, the judge presiding over the counter-
suits between Perdue and Brown, Random House, and Sony
Pictures, read each of the books in question to determine if the
novels were similar enough to enable a trial to proceed. In August
2005, he ruled that the books were sufficiently different from each
other to negate the need for a trial.

■ ■ ■

After his appearance on *Good Morning America* in January
2004 for *The Da Vinci Code* contest, Brown began to turn down
all media interviews and public appearances, except for causes
and groups that were near and dear to him. On May 18, 2004, he
gave a talk at the Capitol Center for the Arts in Concord to benefit the New Hampshire Writers' Project, an organization that
helped him with advice and support from other writers in 1995,

when he first began writing *Digital Fortress*. More than eight hundred readers and media people showed up at the sold-out event, where Dan Brown was greeted like the prodigal son as he stepped up to the podium.

He was stunned by the reaction. "I pictured a small, quaint little room with maybe thirty people in it," he joked. "But I spent many solitary and hungry years as a writer in this state, and I know how hard it is."

Dan Brown's last public book-signing event for *The Da Vinci Code* took place on December 13, 2003, at Water Street Books, the Exeter bookstore that had provided him with much support as a local author from the time that *Digital Fortress* was first published. This particular signing would benefit Families First, the community health care center in Portsmouth that had long been a recipient of Brown's largesse. The author promised to donate the full cover price of each of his four books sold at the event directly to the nonprofit group. The typical wholesale discount for a hardcover book is 50 percent—e.g., for a book with a price of $25, the bookstore receives $12.50 while the publisher would receive $12.50. This meant that Brown himself would be donating the difference between the bookstore's cost and the cover price. And if his past public appearances were any indication, hundreds, if not thousands of books were sold that day and the line ran well down the block.

Interestingly enough, Dan had maintained in interviews through the years that he continued to compose music and write songs while he toiled away on his novels. At the signing, Brown announced he would be unveiling a surprise holiday project for children, *Musica Animalia*, a CD of songs written and sung by Brown himself, with all proceeds, again, going to Families First.

At the time, the signing was billed as "Brown's last public signing for the next fourteen months," which meant that his next novel was scheduled to appear in the late spring of 2005.

But that was not to be. *The Lost Symbol* would not appear for more than four years for a variety of reasons, two of which were very important. First, the backlash from the Catholic Church was unlike anything he expected. Second, the authors of a book that he respected—and even paid homage to in *The Da Vinci Code*— turned on him in a draining court case, which would end up changing his life—and his work—forever.

CHAPTER NINE

BE **CAREFUL**
WHAT YOU **WISH** FOR

JUST AS HE had never envisioned that *The Da Vinci Code* would become a best-seller around the world, Dan Brown certainly didn't expect the critics to react with such antipathy from the time the book was first published. And the vituperation poured out on his novel was astonishing in both its volume and vehemence.

Cardinal Tarcisio Bertone, the archbishop of Genoa, referred to the book as "a sack full of lies." Later, in the fall of 2004, the book was banned in Lebanon, and government security staffers and police informed booksellers and other retailers across the country that the English, French, and Arabic versions of *The Da Vinci Code* had to be permanently taken off the shelves.

"Contrary to what people may believe, I did not write this book to stir up a hornet's nest," said Dan Brown. "We worship the gods of our fathers. It is truly that simple."

He asserts that the majority of his critics have simply missed the entire point of the novel: "Prior to two thousand years ago, we lived in a world of gods and goddesses," said Brown. "Today, we live in a world solely of God. I simply wrote a story that explores how and why this shift might have occurred, what it says about our past and, more importantly, what it says about our future."

The primary accusation that his critics use to lambaste the book was that it contained many factual errors and inaccuracies, which fueled the two dozen books whose primary aim is to debunk these "facts" that Dan Brown asserted were true. His opponents inevitably relied on this tactic in an effort to show that if he got the little things wrong, then the historical truths he presented in the book—that Jesus and Mary Magdalene were husband and wife, for example—must be patently false. In essence, they wanted to cast the veracity of the entire book into question.

When interviewers asked him about the backlash, however, Brown preferred to focus on the positive feedback he'd received.

"I was a little nervous when the book came out because, yes, there are some very controversial ideas put forth in the book," he admitted. "I'm pleased to say that I'm getting letters from priests and a lot of letters from nuns, from pagans and feminists, and life-time Catholics and people who call themselves recovering Catholics, and everybody is excited and positive about the ideas in this book."

At the same time, he admitted that he was shocked at the degree and venom of the criticism leveled toward him. "I have been accused of all sorts of things this year, among other things, of being anti-Christian," he said. "I was raised Christian, and to this day, I try to live my life following the basic tenets of the teachings of Christ. This book is in no way anti-Christian or anti-Catholic. I am a Christian, although perhaps not in the most traditional sense of the word. I consider myself a student of many religions. My book just looks at the Catechism and the history of Christianity through a slightly different lens, that being the exploration of those books of the Bible that did not make it into Constantine's version, the one we read today."

In interviews, he was also careful to regularly assert that the novel he's written and the facts he exposes shouldn't turn people into nonbelievers. For instance, in the book, he asserted that Constantine and his sons edited the Bible in a way that under-scored the divinity of Christ and would bring pagans and Christians together, therefore creating one brand of Christianity, not the several that existed at that time.

"Constantine was a savvy politician and made some decisions to make Christ more divine perhaps on paper than he really was," he said. "This action in no way undermines the beauty of Christ's message or the beauty of the message of the Bible. It's simply a different way of looking at how that story came about."

■ ■ ■

Once it was clear that *The Da Vinci Code* had staying power and would continue to sell, indeed, in even greater numbers than in the first few months of publication, it didn't take long for the first critical books to appear.

Breaking the Da Vinci Code by Darrell L. Bock, *The Da Vinci Deception* by Erwin W. Lutzer, *Cracking Da Vinci's Code*, by James L. Garlow and Peter Jones, and *The Da Vinci Hoax*, by Sandra Miesel and Carl Olson were just a few of the titles that began to flood the market. All in all, approximately two dozen books critical of *The Da Vinci Code* were published, with most covering the same ground: debunking Brown's version of biblical history and backing theirs up by quoting scripture and interviewing other like-minded experts.

Brown's view of these books was rather surprising. "I think they are absolutely wonderful," he said. "The authors and I obviously disagree, but the dialogue that is being generated is powerful and positive. The more vigorously we consider and debate these topics, the better our understanding of our own spirituality."

He admitted that he had never met any authors of these books, but he wouldn't necessarily rule it out. "I assume they're all very nice people with good intentions," he said. "It's important to keep in mind that in the same way I was out on the talk show circuit trying to sell my book, they are now out trying to sell their books, and it is in their best interest to generate as much controversy as possible, often making inflammatory claims."

But *The Da Vinci Code* infuriated so many people that even those who didn't have a book to promote or an agenda or organization to push soon started refuting the assertions and suppositions in Brown's fourth novel.

"One of my critics, a well-spoken gentleman who is a very devout scholar, went on a radio program and said he was there at the calling of God to correct the misperceptions put forth in *The Da Vinci Code*," said Brown. "He told the interviewer he was angry with me for teaching inaccurate history."

Another accusation that his critics leveled at him was that he was a conspiracy theorist, a charge that he flatly denied.

"I am most certainly not a conspiracy theorist," he said. "I can tell you right upfront that I don't believe in extraterrestrials, and I don't believe that crop circles are anything more than a very well-executed joke. And I don't believe in the Bermuda triangle. The story in *The Da Vinci Code* is so well documented historically that the only reason it falls under conspiracy is because we all believe a different truth. And my question is, 'Which conspiracy? Which version of the truth is a conspiracy?'"

As could be expected, the media ate it up, at least for a while. "The media has a very high tolerance for controversy, but even so, all of this refuting and debunking of the novel has gotten so absurd, and in some cases so hateful, that even the media has begun to tire of it," he asserted fourteen months after *The Da Vinci Code* was published.

As far as whether people were making a little bit too much of it, he laughed at a comment that a priest made about the book. "He said that Christian theology has survived the writings of Galileo and the writings of Darwin," said Brown. "Surely it will survive the writings of some novelist from New Hampshire."

Brown asserted that most theologians believe that religion only has one true enemy, and it's not his book, but rather, apathy. "We get so caught up in our lives that we forget to go to church, we forget to go to temple, we forget to think about God, we forget to take time for spirituality," he said. "Apathy has a pretty good antidote, and that is passionate debate. I am thrilled to see there is so much of it. Debate makes us think about what we believe and why we believe it. Debate forces us to actively explore our beliefs, which is invigorating and healthy for religion as a whole."

Of course, the groups that believe they were maligned in *The Da Vinci Code*—whether directly or indirectly—have understandably taken measures to distance themselves from the book, and to condemn Brown's assertion that the historical items in the book are factual.

Opus Dei, the group that perhaps is portrayed in the least flattering light in the novel, immediately denounced the book on its Web site and in the media: "Notwithstanding the book's marketing promotion and its pretension to authentic scholarship, the truth is that the novel distorts the historical record about Christianity and the Catholic Church and gives a wholly unrealistic portrayal of the members of Opus Dei and how they live."

Brown responded, "Any time you have a lot of money and you are secretive about what you do, whether you are the National Security Agency, Opus Dei, or the Vatican, people are going to assume that you are doing the worst." He doesn't paint the group with one big negative brushstroke, however, despite what his critics may think. "At the same time, I have met students and professionals for whom modern religion does not offer the stringency and the structure that they need, and Opus Dei for them has been a powerful and grounding experience," he said.

Some might feel that with all the groups and organizations he's inadvertently offended in his novels, he might need to hire a bodyguard. But he dismisses any concern for his safety. "I work very hard to portray these organizations in a fair and even light, and I think I've succeeded," he said. In addition, he has repeatedly maintained that he believes in everything he presented in *The Da Vinci Code*, including the fact that Jesus and Mary Magdalene were married. "I will say that the Holy Grail as described in the novel I truly believe really exists the way I have described it," he said.

In the very beginning of *The Da Vinci Code*, Dan Brown writes, "All descriptions of artwork, architecture, documents, and secret rituals in this novel are accurate." But interestingly enough, about two months after the release of *The Da Vinci Code*, Brown was starting to back away from his "everything is factual" stance that essentially served as an open invitation to millions of offended Catholics and others to denounce the book.

"Ninety-nine percent of it is true," he said in May 2003.

Even people whose ideas he respected enough to name characters after had their reservations about what Brown did in *The Da Vinci Code*. "We said there is evidence to support these things. But evidence is not the same as proof. Dan Brown is taking it as fact," said Richard Leigh, whose last name Brown adopted as the first name of Leigh Teabing, in *The Da Vinci Code*. Leigh is the coauthor of *The Holy Blood and the Holy Grail*, a book published in the U.K. in 1982 that Brown lists in his bibliography and has described as a major influence.

Even though the sales of Leigh's own book went through the roof as a result of the worldwide visibility brought on by its association with *The Da Vinci Code*, Leigh still complained along with others who had presented these ideas to the public in book form through the years. While their complaints may have been nothing more than sour grapes, the truth is that scholarly books will rarely capture the attention of the world—no matter how shocking or controversial the topic—as much as a tautly written thriller that unfolds over the course of twenty-four hours.

"There are plenty of nonfiction books about these subjects, but not many novels," Brown said. "Many people aren't familiar with them. When you're looking for a beach book, you don't look for a historical tome on the Catholic Church."

As the controversy swirled, Brown returned to one theme again and again: At one point in time, every major world religion had both gods and goddesses as part of its theology, but today most brands of mainstream Christianity celebrate only the male side of the equation, with one God. He believes this imbalance is both a symptom and a cause of society's ills today.

"I think that any one of us who turns on CNN or NPR has a good sense that we are living in a life out of balance," he said. "Every Osiris had his Isis, and every Mars had his Venus. Today we live in a world of just gods. The goddess is gone. And it's interesting to note that the word *god* in modern society conjures up images of piety and of strength and credibility, and yet its counterpart *goddess* sounds like a myth, like a fable."

While his fans found this explanation to be heartening, his critics continued to accuse Brown and his two Robert Langdon novels of atheism, blasphemy, and ultra-liberalism, among other things.

He did his best to take the relentless criticism with a grain of salt. Perhaps he took the most pride in his New Hampshire roots when the cartoonist for the *Union Leader*, the state's largest newspaper with a long-standing conservative reputation, devoted a cartoon to the controversy over *The Da Vinci Code*. Brown joked about it at the talk for the New Hampshire Writers' Project. "A gentleman just patted me on the back and congratulated me on a rather dubious honor, to have been beaten up by the *Union Leader* without even running for office," he said.

After getting lambasted for months about the ideas he presented in his fourth novel, Brown said that not only was his faith not shaken, but that he also had just as many questions about religion and spirituality as before. He admitted that he envies people—critics and fans alike—who are absolutely certain of their faith and where they stand on it. "I really wish I had the luxury of absolute unquestioning faith," he said. "I do not, and I am still searching. I wrote *The Da Vinci Code* as part of my own spiritual quest. I never imagined a novel could become so controversial."

CHAPTER TEN

PULLING BACK
THE CURTAIN

IN OCTOBER 2005, after rebuffing their publisher's request to refrain from legal action—a company that also happened to be the publisher of *The Da Vinci Code* in the U.K.—Leigh and Baigent filed a civil lawsuit against Random House in London, where they accused the publisher—and therefore Brown by extension—of infringing upon their copyright in their bestselling book *The Holy Blood and the Holy Grail*, a book presenting the theory that Jesus did not die on the cross, but instead survived and went on to father children in a bloodline that continues to this day. They also alleged that the outline and architecture Brown employed to structure *The Da Vinci Code* mimicked theirs as well, a point that the plaintiffs would drop midtrial. A third coauthor, Henry Lincoln, declined to participate in the lawsuit, with speculation running from his own ill health to the possibility that he didn't agree with the other two authors' decision to pursue legal action.

The American edition of Leigh and Baigent's book—*Holy Blood, Holy Grail*—was published in 1983. The book met with similar popularity—and derision—as Brown's novel would a full two decades later. After all, the authors were presenting ideas that amounted to heresy and blasphemy, which of course resulted in sending the book rocketing onto best-seller lists, and helping it to remain a steady seller through the years.

Though Brown was not named as a defendant in the lawsuit, Justice Peter Smith of the Royal Courts of Justice declared that

Random House couldn't have defended the case without the author's testimony and witness statement. "In reality," Smith later wrote in his decision, "Mr. Brown is on trial over the authorship of *The Da Vinci Code*."

Even though Smith relished the opportunity to help shed light on the degree to which authors of both nonfiction and fiction can draw on research by other authors in their own work, he began the trial with a somewhat gimlet eye toward the true motivations of both plaintiffs and defendant, given the fact that the international publicity generated by the trial would inevitably increase sales of both books and also help to promote the forthcoming movie based on Brown's novel.

"By virtue of various mergers and acquisitions, Random [House] publishes both *Holy Blood, Holy Grail,* and *The Da Vinci Code*," Smith wrote. "Further, a film production of *The Da Vinci Code* is apparently in the offing starring Tom Hanks with a scheduled release in May 2006. It is a testament to cynicism in our times that there have been suggestions that this action is nothing more than a collaborative exercise designed to maximize publicity for both books.

"I am not in a position to comment on whether this cynical view is correct," he continued, "but I would say that if it was such a collaborative exercise, Mr. Baigent and Mr. Brown both went through an extensive ordeal in cross-examination which they are likely to remember for some time."

A trial was scheduled to start in late February 2006. The plaintiffs asked for damages as well as a cut of Brown's revenue from the book. It was also speculated that if Leigh and Baigent prevailed, *The Da Vinci Code* movie would be delayed.

However, copyright experts showed that the plaintiffs had their work cut out for them.

"Ideas aren't protected under English law," said copyright expert Robin Fry of Beachcroft Wansbroughs, a law firm in London. "The paradox here is that you can have a 600-page book and someone steals one paragraph and that's a copyright breach, but if you steal the whole basis of the book, then that's not a breach."

Rupert Bent, an attorney specializing in intellectual property in Birmingham, U.K., concurred. "Cases involving copyright infringement are notoriously difficult to prove," he said. "The claimant needs to show clear examples of similarities and in most cases, has to narrow these down to specific incidents where an idea has been directly copied."

Regardless of this, writers all over the world were anxious about the case. Julian Barnes, a bestselling contemporary British author who was awarded the Man Booker Prize in 2011, had written several novels that featured historical events, and he was understandably leery of operating in a world where the plaintiffs would prevail, pointing out that Shakespeare relied on history in much the same way as Brown.

"This is how a writer instinctively operates," he said. "It's just the same as if you've been told a story by a friend or something happens in your family. It's all fair game."

Before the trial began, however, both sides got a sneak peek into Brown's life, via a sixty-nine-page witness statement running just over twenty-five thousand words that he wrote to explain how he wrote and researched his novels. He also revealed in great detail the degree to which Blythe was involved in helping to create his thrillers. The big surprise was that Blythe did the lion's share of the research and passed it along to her husband, and that she did so often without including attribution of where a particular fact had come from. Of course, novels don't require footnotes and source citations for every fact mentioned in the book, but once a book becomes world famous and highly controversial, it seems that all bets are off.

At particular issue in the trial were passages and handwritten notes directly written on the pages of the Browns' copy of *Holy Blood, Holy Grail*. Baigent and Leigh accused Brown of relying heavily on their book when creating the outline for his novel; in response, Dan said that theirs was only one of dozens of books consulted over the course of research for the novel, and that Blythe didn't consult their book in the early stages of work on the book. Plus, he maintained that the ideas Leigh and Baigent presented in their book had been readily available in a variety of other sources for decades.

What was clear, however, was that in two years of research for the book, Blythe had generated so much information for her husband to look at that he admitted he easily became overwhelmed at times by the amount of raw data she presented.

"Blythe wrote notes in many of our research books, usually urging me to take note of some interesting fact she had found," wrote Brown, pointing out that his wife had become fascinated by the idea of the Sacred Feminine in the Bible—which eventually led to the explosive story of Jesus and Mary Magdalene revealed in *The Da Vinci Code*—and often pushed Brown to weave even more of the snippets into the novel than he wanted. "She often playfully chided me about my resolve to keep the novel fast-paced, always at the expense of her research. In return, I jokingly reminded her that I was trying to write a thriller, not a history book.

"For every page in each of my novels, I probably wrote ten that ended up in the trash," he admitted. "My tendency toward heavy editing—'trimming the fat,' as I called it—fueled the ongoing push-and-pull between Blythe and me. Blythe constantly urged me to add more facts and more history, while I was always slashing out long descriptive passages in an effort to keep the pace moving. I remember Blythe once gave me an enormous set of architectural and historical notes for a short flashback I was writing about Notre Dame cathedral. When I had finished the section, she was frustrated by how little of her work actually made the final cut. In these situations, I always remind Blythe I was trying to write a fast-moving page-turner."

He also explained how they relied on e-mail to send research and feedback back and forth, which in 2000—when research on the book commenced—was somewhat unusual for the time.

"In the late stages of writing *The Da Vinci Code*, Blythe and I started to use e-mail more frequently to share ideas with each other," he said. "More of our research was taking place on the Internet, and e-mail became the most efficient way of sharing information. For Blythe, sending me cut-and-paste text or a clickable link to a large Web site was easier than printing out dozens of pages in hard copy. For some topics, Blythe pulled together many points and typed up a research document, usually covering the research that I had asked her to do on a particular topic. This new tool of e-mail now meant that those research notes appeared in all kinds of different forms—her own extracts, clips from the Internet, scans from source books, and Web site resource files."

Brown then detailed the final stages of making sense of thousands of pages of information. "I add Blythe's research to my own, and then attempt to distill and make palatable to the reader the raw subject matter," he wrote.

The case opened on February 27, 2006, and hundreds of fans, detractors, and media all wanted a front-row seat at the proceedings.

Much would be revealed in the course of the trial, but perhaps most intriguingly, Brown told how he initially fought the seed of the idea that would serve as the foundation on which he would construct his blockbuster novel.

"This is not an idea that I would ever have found appealing," he admitted. "Being raised a Christian and having sung in my church choir for fifteen years, I'm well aware that Christ's crucifixion is the very core of the Christian faith. Suggesting a married Jesus is one thing, but questioning the resurrection undermines the very heart of Christian belief."

After opening arguments by both sides, the first surprise involved one of the plaintiff's performances on the witness stand, both under cross-examination as well as during questioning by his own attorney. Whether it was from nerves or stage fright, right out of the gate, Baigent proceeded to undermine the points he and Leigh had carefully spelled out in the lawsuit, admitting outright that he had clearly embellished their claims that Brown had plagiarized *Holy Blood, Holy Grail*, which was published as *The Holy Blood and the Holy Grail* in the U.K.

Random House lawyer John Baldwin read aloud a few excerpts from *The Da Vinci Code* and asked Baigent to comment on the supposed similarities between the two books.

"There's no mention of the Priory's oath to keep its true nature hidden in *The Holy Blood and the Holy Grail*, is there?" Baldwin queried.

Baigent replied, "No, I concede that."

"There's no mention of the Priory protecting the tomb of Mary Magdalene, is there?" Baldwin then asked.

"Not explicitly, no," said Baigent.

Attorney Jonathan Rayner James then put his client on the stand, only to be met with similar disastrous results. James would later say that Baigent was "overawed by the circumstances and agreed almost without exception to anything that was said by the judge."

Justice Smith also showed his frustration with Baigent. "He was a thoroughly unreliable witness," he wrote in his ruling. "They say that they do not know whether he was deliberately trying to mislead the court, or was simply deluded and that he is either extremely dishonest or a complete fool. I do not need to decide that issue; it does not matter why he said what he did. I can place no reliance on any part of his evidence."

All eyes were on Brown when he finally took the stand on March 13. During the trial, he wore a dark blue suit with a yellow tie, shedding his usual turtleneck and tweedy professor's blazer.

Attorneys for Baigent and Leigh tried to salvage their case

by going after Brown, but their approach ended up backfiring due to their attention on minutiae. Once he was on the witness stand, Brown's mood alternated between being charming, candid, and frustrated.

He warmed up by talking about how his personality affects his writing. "I have a very short concentration span," he said. "That's why I write in short chapters."

However, his patience and charisma soon wore thin under cross-examination when James dug into bits of paper and jottings that were years old, especially given that he had already admitted to a virtual flood of paper and research materials supplied to him by Blythe. At one point, James pushed Brown to reveal the moment when he learned a detail that would prove critical to his plotting on the novel.

"I couldn't possibly tell you the exact date I learned that Mary Magdalene was not a prostitute," said Brown, his voice rising slightly with frustration.

"It's as if you've asked me to go back five years or ten years and asked me not only what I got for Christmas, but what order I opened the presents."

Another time, James showed that while he had done a great deal of pretrial research, the attorney hadn't done quite enough. When Brown mentioned his hometown bookstore, the Water Street Bookshop in Exeter, James queried if it was "the only bookstore in New Hampshire." Brown cracked up and said, "New Hampshire is a small state, but not *that* small."

At one point on the witness stand, he expressed bewilderment over the fact that he felt the plaintiffs were biting the hand that fed them.

"Baigent and Leigh are only two of a number of authors who have written about the bloodline story, and I went out of my way to mention them for being the ones who brought the theory to mainstream attention," he said.

"For them to suggest that I have 'hijacked and exploited' their work is simply untrue."

During the trial, however, the elephant in the room from both the plaintiffs' legal team and the judge revolved around one question: Where was Blythe Brown? And why didn't she come to London to testify in defense of her husband, especially since, as he had already made clear, she performed the vast bulk of the research not only for *The Da Vinci Code* but for his previous novels as well?

But Dan didn't think it was necessary. "I see no reason why she should be put through the stress that the glare of publicity would cause," he said.

However, during his testimony and his witness statement, Brown made clear that much of the confusion brought up at trial could have been explained by his wife. He denied the role that *Holy Blood, Holy Grail* played in drawing up the outline for *The Da Vinci Code*, but the plaintiff's lawyer pointed to Brown's initial proposal for the book. In it, he included a bibliography of seven books that included *The Templar Revelation*, where the following blurb by author Colin Wilson appeared on the cover: "One of the most fascinating books I have read since *Holy Blood, Holy Grail*."

In addition, Leigh and Baigent's book was mentioned throughout *The Templar Revelation*. Perhaps the most damning piece of evidence appeared on page 39 of the Browns' copy of the book, where James, the plaintiff's attorney, pointed to the following scrawl in the margin alongside the title: *"Get this book."*

Dan had already testified that most of the writing that appeared in the various books and documents that had been presented as evidence had been put there by Blythe. "In my childhood, I was taught never to write in books," he wrote in his witness statement. "To this day, I still have a strong aversion to it. In fact, when I first became published and people asked me to sign their editions, I felt funny about it. For this reason, my margin notes often are very light or taken down on a separate piece of paper. Blythe does not share my idiosyncrasy, and she often marks books very heavily."

This point was amplified in one series of questions by James, when he led Brown through a number of pages in one research book to point out his wife's notes and asked if any were his own. James called his attention to a star in the margin, and proceeded to question Brown if it was Blythe's star, or if she tended toward a different star, and if that was the case, what would that look like? By this point, Brown had had enough.

"A star," he replied, sounding somewhat testy. "A star like anybody would draw."

But Brown then added to the confusion when he said that many of the additional notes that Blythe—and occasionally himself—had written in their copy of *Holy Blood, Holy Grail* actually were made after *The Da Vinci Code* was published. When he made public appearances and signed books in the first month after publication, he was unprepared to deal with the angry people he encountered who challenged him to explain his findings and ask where he did his research. He turned to several books that Blythe had used for research, including *Holy Blood, Holy Grail*.

"I am a novelist, not a historian," he said. "I needed to go back so I could defend the work."

But others weren't so sure his efforts to protect his wife were as innocent as he made it sound, particularly Justice Smith. The trial ended on March 20, 2006, and the judge issued his ruling on April 7. "How *The Da Vinci Code* was researched and created is vital to the issues in this case," he said. "Blythe Brown's role in that exercise is crucial, and I do not accept that there are reasons of a credible nature put forward as to why she has not appeared to give evidence. Accordingly, I conclude that her absence is explicable only on the basis that she would not support Mr. Brown's assertion as to the use made of *Holy Blood, Holy Grail* and when that use occurred in that evidence."

Despite these damning words, the judge then proceeded to let Brown off the hook. "With that in mind, however, I accept Mr. Brown's evidence that he did not *use Holy Blood, Holy Grail* when he wrote the Synopsis," with special emphasis on the word *use*.

Justice Smith then turned his focus on the plaintiffs, declaring that they had failed to prove that Brown had copied the structure and central themes that Leigh and Baigent had used in their book, and that therefore there was no proof of copyright infringement. "Even if the central themes were copied, they are too general or of too low a level of abstraction to be capable of protection by copyright law," he said.

Copyright experts had largely expected the verdict. "Copyright normally works by proving someone else has got the income that you deserved," said Robin Fry. "This is not the case here. I'm sure the Dan Brown book has been a huge boost to sales of *Holy Blood, Holy Grail*. The judge will be influenced by that."

Speaking of money, the judge also seemed to imply that he thought the plaintiffs were greedy. "It is a fact that the claimants' book sales have benefited from *The Da Vinci Code* and this litigation," he said. They had lost the case.

Indeed, the highly visible trial seemed to benefit Leigh and Baigent financially, as both fans and detractors sent the book roaring onto best-seller lists so they could see what all the fuss was about. Amazon announced that sales of *Holy Blood, Holy Grail* increased 3,500 percent after the first day of the trial.

The plaintiffs were clearly dismayed at the judge's decision, not only because they lost but also because they were then responsible for paying the legal costs not only for their attorneys but for Random House's as well, a legal bill estimated at around six million dollars. After the verdict was announced, Baigent sounded as muddled as he did on the stand.

"By its very nature, this case entails a conflict between the spirit and the letter of the law," he said. "I think we lost on the letter. We won on the spirit and to that extent we are vindicated."

Then, in the next breath, a reporter heard him say, "We would have to sell a hell of a lot of books to cover the legal costs."

For the first time since the trial began, when Dan Brown met with reporters after the judge's ruling, he seemed relieved and smiled freely.

"This is a good day both for those who write and for those who enjoy reading," said Brown. "I am still astonished that these two authors chose to file their suit at all. This decision also touches on a wider issue. A novelist must be free to draw appropriately from historical works without fear that he'll be sued and forced to stand in a courtroom facing a series of allegations that call into question his very integrity as a person.

"As J. K. Rowling says, it's like somebody showing up at your door and pointing at your child and saying, 'That's mine.' It's not a pleasant thing to go through, to have all of your work called into question."

■ ■ ■

Brown returned home, and plans for the release of the film version of *The Da Vinci Code* the following month moved forward. Though he had initially resisted selling the movie rights to the blockbuster, he had a change of heart after Ron Howard approached him and tossed the idea of Tom Hanks as Robert Langdon into the mix. Brown reconsidered.

"Part of it was the fact that there was a chance to work with the best of the best," he said. "And part of it was an argument, for better or worse, that there's a whole lot of people who see movies who don't read books, and here is a chance to bring this powerful story to all of those people."

Not to mention that Brown also received six million dollars for the movie rights.

He served as executive producer on the film, and spent some time on the set after production began in late June 2005. He would later admit that it was a difficult transition to make.

"Writing is a solitary existence, while making a movie is controlled chaos—thousands of moving parts and people," he observed. "Every decision is a compromise. If you're writing and you don't like how your character looks or talks, you just fix it. But in a movie, if there's something you don't like, that's tough. And when you make a film, everyone sees the same Harry Potter, the same Robert Langdon. You're all having the same experience—and it may not be what you imagined."

At times, Brown found the experience more than a little surreal. They shot several scenes at the Louvre at night, and one night he was wandering the halls and made his way to the *Mona Lisa*, which he thinks of as "that quietly smiling face who had started this whole thing."

"If that in itself were not enough of a life moment, when I looked out into the grand gallery, I saw an albino monk go running by," he joked. "Needless to say, quite a feeling."

Later, after filming in Edinburgh, he was in a hotel room with Tom Hanks and Ron Howard, as they all got ready for a party where the men had to wear kilts. Brown had never worn one, and Tom Hanks helped him out. Ron Howard asked him, "Dan, when you started writing *The Da Vinci Code*, did you ever imagine you'd be in a hotel room in Scotland with Tom Hanks pinning your skirt?"

"I sheepishly admitted that this exact scenario had been my life dream, and the only way I could get it done was to write *The Da Vinci Code*," he recounted later.

Despite the occasional frivolity, Howard had his doubts before production began. "I was a little daunted," he said. "As soon as I took on the movie, I knew that there was going to be a massive weight of expectation about how it was going to turn out. All I set out to do was to make as faithful an adaptation as I could muster within the framework of what I thought was a good murder mystery with an open-ended resolution. I think I've succeeded in that."

Due to the pent-up demand for the film, along with the increased attention from the recently concluded trial, the movie pulled in $77 million at the box office in the United States the first weekend alone, eventually grossing $217 million in the United States. Plus, its score, by Hans Zimmer, garnered a Golden Globe nomination.

Overall, the critics were not kind. "The Catholic Church has nothing to fear from this film," Anthony Lane of *The New Yorker* wrote. "It is not just tripe. It is self-evident, spirit-lowering tripe that could not conceivably cause a single member of the flock to turn aside from the faith."

Joe Morgenstern at *The Wall Street Journal* concurred: "Even as a visual aid, *The Da Vinci Code* is a deep-dyed disappointment. Paris by night never looked murkier."

■ ■ ■

Brown didn't seem to care. Safely back in New Hampshire, he could finally retreat and relax. After the intrusion and threats of the trial and the hubbub of the movie premiere, both **he** and Blythe needed to hide away from the world for a while.

Especially now that he had revealed himself to the public against his will, which was anathema to his desire for a private life where he could wrestle with demons in his imagination and work side-by-side with his wife without the rest of the world intruding upon his life.

Indeed, many felt that perhaps the most interesting thing to come out of the trial was the peek that his witness statement provided into the hitherto private lives of Dan and Blythe Brown. It would be the closest he would come to writing his autobiography, as he meticulously detailed his work methods and habits, his influences, and how they've evolved and matured through the years.

Above all, the document revealed how they seemingly lived on a secluded island of their own making: traveling and working together in complementary fashion, she the dreamy-eyed researcher, he the cunning novelist executing ultra-detailed outlines and incorporating Blythe's research to spin a highly educational tale of tension and intrigue.

At the trial, they were presented as a united front against not only their accusers but also against the world, which had become more demanding in the wake of their grand success.

But now, they needed their privacy more than ever, for their sanity, security, and most important, so Dan could continue to do what he did best: write blockbusters where he could "mix facts into a fictional setting and get readers to ask questions about what they believe," as he put it. ". . . [And] to make it fun to read. Someone said it's like eating vegetables that taste like ice cream."

Both Dan and Blythe loved visiting islands—Tahiti, Anguilla, and Bali were among a few of their favorites. And so it wasn't long before they proclaimed themselves king and queen of a self-contained island in their beloved New Hampshire, a place that could not be found by anyone, friend or foe, on any map, if they were lucky . . .

CHAPTER ELEVEN

THE ISLE OF
LANGDONIA

AS THESE THINGS go, it probably started as a joke . . . or maybe not. After all, their lives had been radically and permanently changed by the man named Robert Langdon, and he was just as real as the imaginary playmates young Dan had entertained in his mind when he was a boy.

So when Brown mentioned in several media interviews that he and Blythe lived in a place they called the Isle of Langdonia, you knew he wasn't entirely kidding. And they even christened one of their financial accounts The Isle of Langdonia Real Estate Trust.

After the trial was over and the fanfare of the movie debut had died down, he and Blythe retreated to the New Hampshire town of Rye. But as it turned out, it was far from being private enough.

They had bought the three-bedroom English Cotswolds-style cottage located on one acre in Rye in the fall of 2004 for just over $1.6 million. Given the neighborhood, the house wasn't overly ostentatious, though by then he could well afford to buy a more striking house on a cliff overlooking the ocean. He and Blythe happily settled into the neighborhood and joined the Abenaqui Country Club, just a half-mile away, so Dan could work on his golf game. Though the house had intricately landscaped grounds that were specifically designed for privacy, after the stress and uncertainty of the trial, it no longer seemed private enough.

"That lawsuit really kicked a hole in him," said Jim Barrington, a lawyer from Ohio who met him through Mensa, where they were both members, when Brown was working on *Digital Fortress*. "Dan started shutting down."

He even stopped going into town to hang out in his old stomping grounds.

"He used to be kind of like a normal guy," said a shop clerk in Exeter who used to greet him on a regular basis. "Now he's hanging out with Howard Hughes."

Brown put on a brave face for the world. "After devoting so much time and energy to this case, I'm eager to get back to writing my new novel," he announced.

But in order to do that, he had to shut out the world. The stress of the trial and the unwanted attention it brought were likely the impetus for the decision to build a six-foot-high fence of stone and iron around his house. In fact, Rye selectmen called an unscheduled meeting on the same day the trial verdict was announced in London in order to issue a permit for the fence, instead of waiting a couple of weeks until their next regularly scheduled meeting. Construction on the fence began a few days later.

Selectman Craig Musselman would not say if Brown had received recent threats as a result of the trial's outcome, but he and the others didn't hesitate to grant permission for construction to begin immediately. "I think the concern on his part was due to the attention he is getting," said Musselman.

"It sits right out there," said Alan Gould, the police chief of Rye, about Brown's home. "It's a pretty open area . . . and we shared [his] concerns. Whether it's the paparazzi or someone who wants to pour goat's blood on the steps, or just someone who wants a picture, it's our job to offer him and his family the same protection we would anyone else in town."

An unidentified friend told Janice Kaplan of *Parade* magazine that the Browns had received threats ever since *The Da Vinci*

Code was published. "It wasn't quite like the fatwah against Salman Rushdie," said the friend, "but it's been very frightening."

So if the wall made him feel more secure, then that was fine. And once, when he was asked about what he thought the public understood the least when it comes to Dan Brown, he ruefully answered, "Probably my love of privacy."

■ ■ ■

Of course, on the Isle of Langdonia, Blythe is the only other full-time resident. "She is the quiet power behind the throne," said Stan Planton, the Ohio librarian who helped Brown research *Digital Fortress* and who has become a friend.

Perhaps the one aspect of Brown's life that received the most attention during the trial was his relationship with Blythe, mostly because of her previously undisclosed role as his primary researcher, as Brown himself spelled out in his affidavit.

"She is the major researcher and has done most of it from the very beginning," Planton said.

"All my e-mails to Dan were copied to her," he continued. "Dan got all the accolades. Blythe is very defensive of their privacy and did a lot of work that she didn't want to be given the credit for. But she is the major researcher and has done most of it from the very beginning."

Indeed, although the judge painted an unfavorable picture of Blythe during the trial, speculating that perhaps she had something to hide that could have potentially affected the outcome of the trial, others have a different outlook.

"Blythe is open and warmhearted, an excellent chef and painter, and very skilled in many respects," said Planton. "She deserves to take more credit than she is willing to accept."

Another interesting thing became clear during the trial: At some point during their lives on the Isle of Langdonia, Dan and Blythe reversed roles from the years when she was a high-powered music executive and he was the quiet, intellectual songwriter.

Now she stays in the background while he occasionally—albeit reluctantly—surfaces to make the rounds and hang with celebrities. During the trial, she remained behind and allowed her husband to fight the war, while when they first met it was the other way around.

"[Blythe] was everything [Dan] wasn't: an extrovert, a great schmoozer," said Paul Zollo, who worked with Blythe at the National Academy of Songwriters. "She understood how the business worked. At parties, Dan would be shy and stand in a corner by himself. Blythe would be schmoozing, introducing people to him. She was great at all the things he was uncomfortable with. It was clear with Blythe and Dan that commercial success was what they were after."

"She was like the classic pushy mother," said a friend who knew them both during their days in Los Angeles. "She had this overwhelming need to push him onto the stage. It didn't really seem to matter what stage it was. He had the talent, but she had the drive . . . that's what their relationship [was] all about. Even around the dinner table, she would always be priming him to tell this or that anecdote, or talking up his strengths. In many respects, it's more like a mother/son relationship than a marriage."

At the same time, that same friend clearly recognized the strong bond between the couple. "They are truly a gifted team and a perfect couple," he added. "The love between them is something I've rarely witnessed in my lifetime."

Indeed, even today Blythe assumes a bit of the earth mother vibe. Planton's wife, Margaret, told stories of when they would stay at the Rye home to spend a few days with the couple, she and Blythe would head off into the mountains to pick blueberries. Once they returned home, she would immediately set about making pancakes or muffins with their finds.

These days, however, Brown doesn't need Blythe to stand up for him any longer. You can even see the change in recent TV interviews and appearances: Dan appears confident, more self-assured than his earlier appearances, when sometimes he came to resemble a deer in the headlights when faced with an onslaught of reporters and photographers.

"They say Bill Clinton has that quality, the ability to make you feel like you're the only person in the room," said Barrington. "Dan is like that."

The fence was up, the legal battles were over. Dan could now happily retreat in peace to resume work on his next book, which he'd already hinted would be about the Freemasons. However, it soon turned out that the six-foot-high fence and state-of-the-art security system to protect the Isle of Langdonia clearly would not be enough. The constant barrage of fans driving by the house and wandering through neighbors' backyards to try to catch a glimpse of the man or the cottage out back where he worked still continued. And though they were shielded from most of the threats, even one unwanted hazard to their safety was one too many.

"On some level, I've met some wonderful people," he admitted. "It's not all nutcases, but there [have] been concerns and issues with security. It's not all puppies and rainbows."

And so Dan and Blythe moved even farther away from the world. They decided on a retreat in the woods where they could create the home of their dreams, while also enjoying adequate privacy without having to resort to twenty-four-hour armed guards at the entrance to the property.

They bought a one-hundred-year-old hunting lodge and proceeded to remodel and then build onto it to create the kind of house where their isle's namesake would feel right at home. Brown described the new addition as "the kind of house Langdon would love. It's filled with secret tunnels, revolving bookcases, and codes and symbols built into the interior woodwork."

The house also features a sizable library that Brown likes to refer to as the "Fortress of Gratitude," as it contains at least one copy of every edition of his five novels, which have been published in fifty-two languages. Shelves in the "fortress" also hold props from the movies made from his books, including the cryptex from *The Da Vinci Code* and a small vial of antimatter from *Angels & Demons*, which would be released in 2009. They moved into the new remodeled house around the end of 2009, just as he finished his months-long world tour to promote *The Lost Symbol*.

The house is equipped with an extensive security system, and there's a corner in the cottage where he can hang from his gravity boots, which he still uses to puzzle out a tough plot point during a writing session, though he quickly brushes aside any comparison to the movie star who first popularized them in *American Gigolo* way back in 1980.

"I wish I *looked* like Richard Gere in the gravity boots," he said. "The gravity boots are terrific because they not only increase your circulation to your head, you really think differently upside down. I have this habit of painting Langdon into a spot, and just saying, 'You know what? I know I'm gonna find a way out of this.' And then if you don't, you've got to hang upside down and think about it from a different point of view. And sometimes it works."

So the house has served as somewhat of a return to his days of anonymity, when he could write in peace. However, it's clear he's happy to leave some parts of the old days behind. "When I published *Angels & Demons*, I would go to bookstores and give talks, and there would be five or six people in the audience. And three of them were bookstore owners who had taken off their badges so I wouldn't feel bad," he said. "When *The Da Vinci Code* came out, I was suddenly talking to 300 or 400 people."

In a way, by creating the Isle of Langdonia, Dan Brown was only retreating to an earlier, happier, less-complicated time: his childhood. "I was a shy kid," he admitted. "I grew up without television. I had a dog, and we lived up in the White Mountains in the summer, and I had no friends up there. And I would just go play hide-and-seek with my dog and probably had some imaginary friends. But it worked."

CHAPTER TWELVE

LIFE ON HIS TERMS

THE YEARS 2007 and 2008 were relatively quiet for Dan and Blythe Brown, a fact that they relished. After all, since the publication of his blockbuster fourth novel, he had faced one interruption after another, without an uninterrupted block of time to work on his new book.

Now, with the trial and movie debut behind him, he would get his chance to dig into his writing. Of course, the moment he dropped out of the public eye, the public at large—his critics as well as his fans—began to wonder what was wrong, and when his next novel would appear.

For Brown's publisher, the novel couldn't come soon enough. In October 2008, Doubleday cut 10 percent of its staff across the board, though the company publicly said that the fact that there was no new Dan Brown novel was not the cause. "I don't think it had anything to do with Dan," said his editor Jason Kaufman in 2009. "People are forgetting that publishing was in a really, really bad place at the end of last year. Is Dan Brown going to save publishing? It's preposterous, and no one person can do that. But there's no question the pressure was on."

But booksellers were getting annoyed at the delay. Jeffrey A. Trachtenberg, who covers book publishing at *The Wall Street Journal*, reported as such. "The whole industry is impatient," he wrote. "Book sales are generally sluggish, and one explosive, high-profile title can jump-start sales across the board as customers

pour into the stores and walk out with a bagful of titles." He pointed out that when parent company Bertelsmann AG announced
its 2007 revenue statement in March 2008, it would be the first
time in five years that the publisher did not experience a significant lift from sales of *The Da Vinci Code*.

"When a major author doesn't deliver, you get down on your
knees and pray," said Laurence Kirshbaum, a former book agent
in New York who is now a publisher. "You can't threaten, you
can't cajole, you wait.

"When you have that level of success, you feel an obligation.
He's climbing Everest times ten. He probably wants to make the
next book perfect."

Brown concurred. "Those little quips of [Langdon's] that
refer to some obscure fact from the thirteenth century just roll off
his tongue, but it takes me a day or two to write one," he said. "I
had a lot to learn and read and get my head around, and to reveal
it, in a fictional chase.

"I'm in no hurry," he added. "I just have to write a great
follow-up and it'll be done when it's done.

"I will not write a lame follow-up. It could take me twenty
years. But I will never turn in a book that I'm not happy with. Four
years ago I wasn't happy with the book. Five years ago I wasn't
happy with the book. And if the book weren't good, I'd be terrified.

"This novel has been a strange and wonderful journey," he
said. "Weaving five years of research into the story's twelve-hour
time frame was an exhilarating challenge. Robert Langdon's life
clearly moves a lot faster than mine."

As it turned out, the book almost didn't happen. Unbeknownst to most, for the first time in his life, Dan Brown encountered a crippling case of writer's block. It threw him for a loop,
because ever since childhood, the words always just poured out
of him.

"When I was five years old, my mother helped me write and
publish my first book," he recalled. "I dictated, she transcribed, and

we did a print run of one with a cardboard cover and a yarn bind-ing. I titled this thriller *The Giraffe, the Pig, and the Pants on Fire*.

"I could barely write my own name back then, but I could, however, make up stories," he continued. "I remember my moth-er's patient hand as she dutifully wrote down every word I uttered. I remember the excitement I felt to see my story expand-ing across sheet after sheet of white paper. I remember dictating the last words of my grand finale and then emblazoning the book's final page with two hardly legible words—Danny Brown—in bright red Crayola crayon."

However, after *The Da Vinci Code*, Brown's always reliable writing life ran into a few obstacles.

He and Blythe were already working on his fifth novel—what would eventually be published in 2009 as *The Lost Symbol*—when *The Da Vinci Code* was published. "There was a vast ocean of time between [the two novels]," he explained. "My life changed dramatically and Blythe and I had to get used to a much different life.

"The thing that happened to me—and must happen to any writer who's had success—is that I temporarily became very self-aware," he continued. "Instead of writing and saying, 'This is what the character does,' you say, 'Wait, millions of people are going to read this.' It's sort of like a tennis player who thinks too hard about a stroke—you're temporarily crippled."

Brown eventually overcame this obstacle through a combi-nation of time passing as well as immersing himself in the story. "The furor died down, and I realized that none of it had any rel-evance to what I was doing," he said. "I'm just a guy who tells a story."

But there was undoubtedly another reason as well: As a result of the copyright infringement lawsuit, even though the judge had ruled in his favor, the fact was that the murkiness of Blythe's past research had attracted notice during the trial. Now, Brown and his wife had to conduct their research much more carefully, meticulously documenting every fact and snippet he would go on to incorporate into his novel, no matter how small.

Plus, there was speculation that the 2007 movie about the Freemasons, *National Treasure: Book of Secrets*, covered much of the same ground as his future novel, which may have driven him to revamp the story line of the book.

In addition, Brown probably lost a few nights of sleep when Baigent and Leigh found a British court to consider an appeal in their case of copyright infringement. Luckily, the appeals judge upheld Justice Smith's original ruling. "Common sense and justice have prevailed, helping to ensure the future of creative writing in the U.K.," said Gail Rebuck, CEO at Random House U.K. "We believe that the case should never have come to court in the first place. Misguided claims like the one that we have faced, and the appeal, are not good for authors and not good for publishers."

Sadly, Leigh died later that year, in November, at the age of sixty-four. More than a few speculated that the stress of the trial and the subsequent appeal contributed to his death from a heart condition.

■ ■ ■

The movie version of *Angels & Demons* was released on May 15, 2009. Once again, Brown served as executive producer on the film.

Ron Howard and Tom Hanks both returned. This time, Howard had to get creative, since the Vatican had banned TV and film crews from shooting inside Roman churches in the wake of the uproar after the *Da Vinci Code* movie. So he had no choice but to build movie sets that looked like St. Peter's Square and the Basilica, among other iconic Vatican buildings.

But another wrench was thrown into the mix. Usually, whenever the Vatican refused permission to a film crew to use the actual churches, they often provided after-hours access to the buildings so the filmmakers could take detailed photographs with specially calibrated large-scale cameras that would help them to construct the sets.

However, the Vatican refused to allow Howard even that, as they were incensed by Brown's view of Biblical history as presented in *The Da Vinci Code*.

"The ban really put us in a lot of trouble because we could not use the precision instruments which are used to take photographs and make reconstructions in the computer," explained special effects director Ryan Cook.

Howard shed some additional light on the matter. "We didn't shoot at the Vatican . . . *officially*," he said. "But cameras can be made really small."

Cook explained how it worked: "For weeks we sent in a team of people to mix with tourists and take 250,000 photographs and hours of video footage," he said, explaining that he and his team then culled through the photographs and videos to create sets and digitally alter scenes in the film.

For his part, Hanks was glad to be back in the role of Brown's alter ego, admitting that he identified with the character. "Like Langdon, I love a game of logic that can only be solved with a combination of lateral thinking and knowledge of the facts," he said. "[Also] like Langdon, I always want to win. Unlike Langdon, I'm usually in third or fourth place. That differentiates me from Robert."

In fact, he started to sound a lot like Langdon's creator when talking about his reasoning for repeating the role: "When I go to church, and I do, I ponder the mystery. I meditate on the 'why.' Why bad things happen to good people and good things happen to bad people.

"Both science and religion speak in a different language, but every now and again they hit on the same subject," he continued. "We are all the same thing, we're all just one."

When asked if he'd be making an appearance in the inevitable movie made from *The Lost Symbol*, he had this to say: "I'm not going to give up on this gig, it's an awfully good job. I'm not going to hand it over to someone else—I'm not stupid!"

Angels & Demons grossed just over $46 million in its opening weekend in the United States, pulling in $133 million at the box office overall. But as before, the critics weren't thrilled. Peter Rainer of *The Christian Science Monitor* said, "*Angels & Demons* is an OK action film, but only the humorless will find it heretical—or educational." Critic Michael Phillips at the *Chicago Tribune* gave it only 1½ stars: "The major players are back for more grandiloquent hackery," he wrote. "Hanks returns to the dullest role of his career, under the direction of Howard, who takes the material as seriously as a kidney stone on the way out."

■ ■ ■

In the spring of 2009, not only did *Angels & Demons* open in movie theaters around the world, but Doubleday announced that Brown's long-awaited novel, *The Lost Symbol*—a change in title from the original *Solomon's Key*—would be published on September 15 of that year. Brown hinted that the exact date was carefully chosen in accordance with his habit of developing codes—on TV shows, on the cover, and now revolving around the publication date—in connection with his novels.

Some noted that the numbers in the date 9/15/09 added up to 33, which they speculated would turn out to be an important number in the novel. But perhaps more important, it is the anniversary of a key day in Masonic history. On September 15 in 1793, the cornerstone was laid at the U.S. Capitol, after President George Washington—a Mason himself—led a parade of Freemasons down Pennsylvania Avenue.

Fans also wondered: Why did Brown pick the Freemasons?

Harkening back to his childhood, Brown described one of his earliest observations of the group back in Exeter: "Their lodge was above the theater, and the shades were always drawn," he explained, as if no more words were necessary.

However, in digging into his real motivations, he appeared to be interested in profiling a more inclusive type of secret society than the one examined in *The Da Vinci Code*.

"In a world where men do battle over whose definition of God is most accurate, I cannot adequately express the deep respect and admiration I feel toward an organization in which men of differing faiths are able to 'break bread together' in a bond of brotherhood, friendship, and camaraderie," he wrote in a letter to the Freemasons just after the book's publication.

He then emphasized his position to make sure there was no confusion over his statement: "It is my sincere hope that the Masonic community recognizes *The Lost Symbol* for what it truly is: an earnest attempt to reverentially explore the history and beauty of Masonic Philosophy."

On the day of publication, Brown explained his motivations to Matt Lauer in greater detail. "[The Masons] are fascinating because we live in a world where different cultures are killing each other over whose version of God is accurate," he said. "And here you have an organization, a global organization, that is spiritual and yet will bring Muslims, Jews, Christians and even just people that are confused about their religion, bring them together and say, 'Look, we all agree that there's some good, big thing out there. But we're not going to put a label on it. Let's worship together.'

"The mystery is in their origins, and in the fact that they have managed to remain pretty secret," he continued. "Their rituals are arcane. And you sort of catch snippets of what the rituals are like. And you can really see a lot of what happens within the organization."

He offered up this intriguing nugget when a reporter asked if he ever thought of joining the Masons. After stating that he believed the group offered up a "beautiful blueprint for human spirituality," he regretted that there was no way that he could become a member. "If you join the Masons, you take a vow of secrecy," he said. "I could not have written this book if I were a Mason."

An added bonus was that much of Freemasonry's history took place in Washington, D.C., an important point since setting has played an important part in all of his novels to date. Plus, he had long been fascinated by the hidden aspects of the nation's capital.

"Washington, D.C., has everything that Rome, Paris, and London have in the way of great architecture: obelisks and pyramids and underground tunnels and great art and a whole shadow world that we really don't see," he said.

Of course, once the publication date was announced, the frenzy among fans and critics was immediate, and only increased as September 15 grew closer.

Two weeks before the official release of the book, Doubleday's warehouse was filled with over five million copies and was manned by armed guards around the clock. One week before the launch, the publisher had essentially locked its doors against the world in order to prevent any copies of the book from getting into the wrong hands. Even book reviewers had to go to unusual lengths in order to read the book: First, they were required to sign a nondisclosure agreement, then they had to surrender their cell phones, and finally, agree to read the 509-page book in one sitting.

"You do not want to be caught stealing this book," Brown quipped about the careful preparations.

After the book came out, there was no angry reaction and pointing out of mistakes and egregious errors like he had encountered after the publication of *The Da Vinci Code*.

Instead, some critics focused on what they saw as a curiously deadened story line and cardboard characters, as well as the fact that Brown seemed like he had gone easy on the group. Some wags inevitably commented that this may be due to his desire to sign up with the Masons in the future and not wanting to alienate them.

But others felt that Brown had delivered, and the book broke the first-day sales record for adult fiction at both Amazon and Barnes & Noble.

In *Newsweek*, reviewer Malcolm Jones had this to say: "Reading *The Lost Symbol* may be more like working a great crossword puzzle than reading *War and Peace*, but that doesn't mean it's not a fascinating pleasure . . . Brown is a maze maker who builds a puzzle and then walks you through it. His genius lies in uncovering odd facts and suppressed history, stirring them together into a complicated stew and then saying, *what if?*"

"Brown's narrative moves rapidly, except for those clunky moments when people sound like encyclopedias," wrote Nick Owchar in the *Los Angeles Times*. "But no one reads Brown for style, right? The reason we read Dan Brown is to see what happens to Langdon."

Over at *The New York Times*, unlike her colleague Janet Maslin, who had helped launch Brown's fourth novel into the world with eloquent and wild praise, *The Lost Symbol* reviewer Maureen Dowd appeared to be unimpressed. "Emotions are the one thing Dan Brown can't seem to decipher," she wrote. "His metaphors and similes thud onto the page . . . In the end, as with *The Da Vinci Code*, there's no payoff. Brown should stop worrying about unfinished pyramids and worry about unfinished novels."

But Brown wasn't swayed by these reviews. He was probably most eager to hear the reaction from the Freemasons themselves.

"We are very pleased [with the book]," said Greg Levenston, Grand Master of the United Grand Lodge of New South Wales and Australian Capital Territory. "There is nothing in this book that will offend my organization. It does give us the opportunity to open it up a bit."

For his part, Brown took a prosaic view of the book's publication, saying that his experiences since *The Da Vinci Code* was published six and a half years earlier had changed him. "I've been through a lot," he said. "I've thought a lot about life, and I've spent a lot of time studying history and science. The theme of this book has a lot to do with the power of our thoughts. And I have great hope for the future and try to nudge the future with this book in certain directions.

"My faith is a work in progress," he continued. "The more I learn, the more I realize I don't know. So it's a catch-22, you keep exploring, and the more you learn, the more you realize you're just lost. It's a very strange world out there."

Perhaps he was most surprised to discover that his religious views were shifting beneath his feet. "The irony is that I've really come full circle," he said. "The more science I studied, the more I saw that physics becomes metaphysics and numbers become imaginary numbers. The farther you go into science, the mushier the ground gets. You start to say, 'Oh, there is an order and a spiritual aspect to science.'"

■ ■ ■

After *The Lost Symbol* was published and after making the requisite publicity tours around the world, Brown once again retreated to the Isle of Langdonia to resume work on what would become his sixth novel, and his fourth featuring Robert Langdon.

He'd occasionally surface in public to do some research or take advantage of his fame by calling upon a few high-profile fans of his work to help him out. Besides the money, one of the upsides of being a celebrity—albeit a reluctant one—was using his visibility to gain access to inner circles that are rarely visited by laypeople.

"One of the great luxuries of having written *The Da Vinci Code* is that it gave me access to all kinds of things I never had access to before," he said. "You have access, and simultaneously, you often need to do your research in other ways, under other names or through other routes."

For instance, to research *The Lost Symbol*, he relied on former New Hampshire senator Judd Gregg to give him an insider's tour of the U.S. Capitol. When they stepped out onto the enclosed skywalk that goes around the dome of the building, rising 180 feet above the rotunda and typically only open to members of Congress, Brown froze with a combination of claustrophobia and his crippling fear of heights. "It was absolutely terrifying," he said.

At other times, however, he prefers to go undercover for his research. When he visited the House of the Temple, a Masonic building in Washington, he signed up for the public tour disguised as a noncelebrity. "I went in a hat and glasses and with a notebook," he said.

■ ■ ■

Dan and Blythe Brown settled into their new home and started working together to create the next best-seller featuring Robert Langdon. Speculation about Brown's activities and whereabouts would occasionally surface—as it did in December 2010 when news hit that he was working on the screenplay for *The Lost Symbol*, a distraction from novel writing that lasted little more than a year, when Sony Pictures announced in March 2012 that seasoned screenwriter Danny Strong had replaced him on the project—but happily, for the most part, the world left them undisturbed.

It was as if they'd struck a deal with the universe: *If you'll just leave us alone, you'll get the next book a lot faster.*

Then, in January of 2013, word arrived about his next novel, along with a confirmed publication date.

Inferno would be published on May 14, 2013. Early buzz in the industry was that Brown had returned to his *Da Vinci Code* roots, making the novel edgier than *The Lost Symbol*, which was sure to incense people around the globe and of course, boost sales.

"Although I studied Dante's *Inferno* as a student, it wasn't until recently, while researching in Florence, that I came to appreciate the enduring influence of Dante's work on the modern world," Brown said in announcing the book's release. "With this new novel, I am excited to take readers on a journey deep into this mysterious realm . . . a landscape of codes, symbols, and more than a few secret passageways."

The difference this time around was that Brown knew exactly how to handle the announcement and fame. Indeed, he had matured, scarred by the scathing reactions to *The Da Vinci Code* and then again by the betrayal and intrusion of the U.K. trial. It was obvious in his public appearances that he was more polished than before and less off-the-cuff. He was no longer an unknown novelist launching his fourth novel out into the world in a last-ditch effort at success.

Then again, there are people who say that he hasn't changed one bit. "He is the same person he [always] was," said his editor Jason Kaufman. "It's harder for him to walk down the street, but he is remarkably levelheaded about his life."

"I wouldn't describe him as especially driven," said Doubleday president Stephen Rubin, who is now president of Henry Holt. "He's very focused. He's an extremely charming, very smart, preppy guy, like the college professor you never had. He's impossible not to like."

And he still writes first thing in the morning in an office that lacks a phone and Internet connection. "My writing process remains unchanged. I still get up at four a.m. every morning and face a blank computer screen. My current characters really don't care how many books I've sold, and they still require my same effort and cajoling to persuade them to do what I want."

As always, Dan credits his wife with helping him keep things in perspective. "Blythe is a wonderfully grounding force, and she told me long before this book came out—when we sensed that it might be a hit—she said, 'I don't care if it hits number one, you're still taking out the trash,'" he joked.

Does he plan to remain in his native New Hampshire? Most likely. The state has undoubtedly treated him well and has served as a good home base. People in the Granite State tend to treat those who the rest of the world thinks of as superstars as just regular people.

"The state is a cultural mecca for a lot of writers and artists, but it's hidden," said Brendan Tapley, communications director for the MacDowell Colony in Peterborough, New Hampshire, an internationally known writers' retreat. "What draws writers here is the degree to which this area seems to respect them as artists while leaving them alone. You're coming up against the classic New England sensibility where you don't tout what you do."

Dan Brown is presently the state's biggest celebrity. But despite the fact that *Da Vinci Code* tours of the Louvre and Rome are making guides big bucks, in this private part of the world, no one yet has set up shop in Exeter to offer guided tours of his hometown: "This is where Dan Brown attended nursery school. . . . Our next stop will be the tennis court at Phillips Exeter where Dan Brown played regularly . . ."

And what of *Inferno*? Almost certainly, it will set new records and send millions of readers to the store the first day it's out to eagerly devour it, studying the clues and codes on the pages within, and perhaps on the cover. They'll expect to learn about new facts that would ordinarily never cross their path, all conjured up in a unique mix of thriller and college lecture.

It's safe to say that any book that comes from Brown's pen from now until the end of his life will be met with fanfare—and backlash—that is rarely seen for any author. "Nobody likes to be attacked," he says. "But when you write books whose premise is that the history that we know isn't the full story, those who have embraced that history won't be happy."

But with all that he's experienced, he's finally become comfortable with that. "I set out to write the kind of book that I want to read," he said. "My goal was that you get to the last page having had a great time, and after you close the cover, you realize, 'Wow, think of everything I have learned.'"

NOTES

PROLOGUE

"I worked very hard . . .": NBC's *Today*, June 9, 2003.

CHAPTER ONE: OF SECRET CODES AND SECRET SOCIETIES

"I grew up in . . .": ABC's *Good Morning America*, November 3, 2003.

"I also grew up . . .": *The Front Porch*, New Hampshire Public Radio, April 23, 2003.

"Gee, I hope not . . .": ABC's *Good Morning America*, November 3, 2003.

"I grew up surrounded . . .": bookreporter.com, March 20, 2003.

"When I was ten years old . . .": *Daily Telegraph* (U.K.), October 2, 2004.

"It was a really great . . .": interview with Susan Ordway, April 2005.

"they take pride in . . .": D. Quincy Whitney, " 'Death of Privacy' Inspires 1st Novel." *The Boston Globe*, July 19, 1998.

"I described with inexhaustible . . .": "Remembered Teachers." *The Boston Globe*, September 29, 1996.

"Since I grew up . . .": New Hampshire Writers' Project talk, May 18, 2004.

"I've always known . . .": bookreviewcafe.com.

CHAPTER TWO: LEAVING THE NEST

"When I graduated from college . . .": Claire E. White, Interview with Dan Brown. writerswrite.com, May 1998.

"We went to thirteen . . .": Amherst College News Service, February 25, 1998, and October 22, 2001.

"To art historians out there . . .": *Weekend Edition*, National Public Radio, April 26, 2003.

"People ask . . .": *Rockingham County Newspapers*, January 19, 1990.

"Parent-teacher conferences . . .": *Calendar*, 1992.

"I remember that Dan . . .": Paul Zollo, personal interview.

"I always wondered . . .": Ron Wallace, personal interview.

"Exeter vaccinated me . . .": *Phillips Exeter Bulletin*, Fall 1992.

"Most of what Exeter . . .": ibid.

"In a field glorifying . . .": ibid.

"I find that teaching . . .": *Calendar*, 1992.

"I remember . . .": Paul Zollo, personal interview.

"People always assume . . .": Susan Winter, personal interview.

"He could have been . . .": Ron Wallace, personal interview.

"Do I really look . . .": *Calendar*, 1992.

"If you pick . . .": Ron Wallace, personal interview.

"She's smart, funny, creative . . .": *Calendar*, 1992.

"We're planning . . .": ibid.

"I'm writing a new . . .": ibid.

"While vacationing in Tahiti . . .": *The Guardian* (U.K.), August 6, 2004.

CHAPTER THREE: PLOTTING THE FUTURE

"I felt funny . . .": Paul Zollo, personal interview.

"It was a silly . . .": bookreviewcafe.com.

"My first reaction . . .": *Union Leader*, March 10, 1998.

"I couldn't help . . .": *Union Leader*, January 18, 1998.

"The NSA's supercomputers . . .": *Union Leader*, January 18, 1998.

"The agency functions . . .": writerswrite.com, May 1998.

"Most cryptography was . . .": *The Boston Globe*, July 19, 1998.

"but the second . . .": ibid.

"If I'm not . . .": *The Front Porch*, New Hampshire Public Radio, April 23, 2003.

"It's essentially a . . .": *The Boston Globe*, July 19, 1998.

"Writing requires . . .": *New Hampshire Magazine*, October 2003.

"The stories are very . . .": Craig McDonald, modestyarbor.com archived Web site.

"Every new technology . . .": angelsanddemons.com archived Web site.

"It's important to remember . . .": ibid.

"The toughest part . . .": writerswrite.com, May 1998.

"I know I am . . .": *The Guardian*, August 6, 2004.

"I read almost exclusively . . .": bookreviewcafe.com.

"I suppose discussing . . .": writerswrite.com, May 1998.

"I was exceptionally lucky . . .": Craig McDonald, modestyarbor .com archived Web site.

"Dan was the writer . . .": Jake Elwell, personal interview.

"The term *audience* . . .": angelsanddemons.com archived Web site.

"I later learned . . .": ibid.

"The most secure area . . .": Craig McDonald, modestyarbor.com archived Web site.

"If you're writing . . .": writerswrite.com, May 1998.

"I'm far more . . .": ibid.

"I am constantly . . .": *New Hampshire Magazine*, October 2003.

"I know where to look . . .": Associated Press, July 14, 2004.

"The message I want . . .": ibid.

"No amount of willpower . . .": Dorothy-L Usenet post, February 21, 1998.

"I am not one . . .": ibid.

"He is a terrific guy . . .": alt.books.review Usenet post, February 2, 2000.

CHAPTER FOUR: A FALSE START

"I would be very surprised . . .": *Union Leader*, March 10, 1998.

"I personally enjoy reading . . .": writerswrite.com, May 1998.

CHAPTER FIVE: UNCERTAIN DAYS

"There's a cybercafe . . .": *Weekend Edition*, National Public Radio, April 26, 2003.

"In many ways . . .": angelsanddemons.com archived Web site.

"It's a great resource . . .": ibid.

"For me . . .": ibid.

"*Deception Point* was set . . .": *The Front Porch*, New Hampshire Public Radio, April 23, 2003.

"Langdon is the man . . .": *Associated Press*, June 9, 2003.

"Langdon is a character . . .": Craig McDonald, modestyarbor .com archived Web site.

"I think he embodies . . .": *The Guardian*, August 6, 2004.

"There are many people . . .": *Weekend Edition*, National Public Radio, April 26, 2003.

"He was fascinated . . .": CNN *Sunday Morning*, May 25, 2003.

"Da Vinci was . . .": ibid.

"Surprisingly, despite Leonardo's . . .": New Hampshire Writers' Project talk, May 18, 2004.

"Chances are I don't. . . .": Craig McDonald, modestyarbor.com archived Web site.

CHAPTER SIX: LAST CHANCE

"I instantly knew . . .": Craig McDonald, modestyarbor.com archived Web site.

"My wife is . . .": ibid.

"There are days . . .": ibid.

"You can't research . . .": *New Hampshire Magazine*, October 2003.

"I began the . . .": ABC's *Good Morning America*, January 12, 2004.

"I was troubled . . .": New Hampshire Writers' Project talk, May 18, 2004.

"Many historians now believe . . .": writerswrite.com, May 1998.

"I think as . . .": Associated Press, June 9, 2003.

"Writing an informative . . .": bookreporter.com, March 20, 2003.

"I very liberally . . .": NBC's *Today*, June 9, 2003.

"I worked very hard . . .": ibid.

"We were given access . . .": *The Front Porch*, New Hampshire Public Radio, April 23, 2003.

"After writing three books . . .": ibid.

"A lot of people . . .": ibid.

"On reflection . . .": Associated Press, July 14, 2004.

"I really got the sense . . .": Craig McDonald, modestyarbor.com archived Web site.

"*The Da Vinci Code* describes . . .": New Hampshire Writers Project talk, May 18, 2004.

"My wife, Blythe . . .": ibid.

"I'm glad I'm not . . .": *The Wall Street Journal*, May 4, 2005.

"The first thing Jason . . .": *The Boston Globe*, May 8, 2004.

"But I thought . . .": ibid.

CHAPTER SEVEN: CHANGING FORTUNES

"A few months before . . .": Associated Press, June 9, 2003.

"We had to find . . .": *The Boston Globe*, May 8, 2004.

"People called and said . . .": Craig McDonald, modestyarbor .com archived Web site.

"Kids have really reacted . . .": ibid.

"We were out of our minds . . .": *The Boston Globe*, May 8, 2004.

"We always acknowledged . . .": *The Guardian*, August 6, 2004.

"It's a thriller . . .": *The Boston Globe*, May 8, 2004.

"I would love to say . . .": *Weekend Edition*, National Public Radio, April 26, 2003.

"The book incorporates . . .": *New Hampshire Magazine*, October 2003.

CHAPTER EIGHT: RUNAWAY SUCCESS

"It's entirely shocking . . .": NBC's *Today*, June 9, 2003.

"There may be more . . .": ABC's *Good Morning America*, January 12, 2004.

"Follow down to the word . . .": ibid.

"All these people . . .": *Publishers Weekly*, April 26, 2004.

"Success has made . . .": ibid.

"We go over every . . .": *The New York Times*, March 21, 2005.

"I have no idea . . .": ibid.

"The positive response . . .": NBC's *Today*, June 9, 2003.

"As far as my . . .": *The Front Porch*, New Hampshire Public Radio, April 23, 2003.

"I had assumed . . .": ibid.

"That's about all . . .": Craig McDonald, modestyarbor.com archived Web site.

"I've never had . . .": *New Hampshire Magazine*, October 2003.

"Because Langdon is . . .": Craig McDonald, modestyarbor.com archived Web site.

"Hollywood has a way . . .": ibid.

"Apparently this happens . . .": NBC's *Today*, June 9, 2003.

"All I can really . . .": NBC's *Today*, June 9, 2003.

"I pictured a small . . .": New Hampshire Writers' Project talk, May 18, 2004.

CHAPTER NINE: BE CAREFUL WHAT YOU WISH FOR

"sack full of lies . . .": *The New York Times*, March 21, 2005.

"Contrary to what people . . .": New Hampshire Writers' Project talk, May 18, 2004.

"Prior to two thousand years . . .": ibid.

"I was a little nervous . . .": *Weekend Edition*, National Public Radio, April 26, 2003.

"I have been accused . . .": New Hampshire Writers' Project talk, May 18, 2004.

"I was raised Christian . . .": bookreporter.com, March 20, 2003.

"My book just looks . . .": *The Front Porch*, New Hampshire Public Radio, April 23, 2003.

"Constantine was a savvy . . .": ibid.

"I think they are absolutely . . .": New Hampshire Writers' Project talk, May 18, 2004.

"I assume they're all . . .": ibid.

"One of my critics . . .": ibid.

"I am most certainly . . .": *The Front Porch*, New Hampshire Public Radio, April 23, 2003.

"The media has a . . .": New Hampshire Writers' Project talk, May 18, 2004.

"He said that Christian . . .": ibid.

"We get so caught . . .": ibid.

"Any time you have . . .": *The Front Porch*, New Hampshire Public Radio, April 23, 2003.

"I work very hard . . .": Craig McDonald, modestyarbor.com archived Web site.

"I will say that . . .": *The Front Porch*, New Hampshire Public Radio, April 23, 2003.

"Ninety-nine percent of it . . .": *CNN Sunday Morning*, May 25, 2003.

"We said there is . . .": NBC's *Today*, October 27, 2003.

"There are plenty of . . .": *Union Leader*, April 23, 2003.

"I think that any . . .": *The Front Porch*, New Hampshire Public Radio, April 23, 2003.

"A gentleman just patted . . .": New Hampshire Writers' Project talk, May 18, 2004.

"I really wish . . .": ibid.

CHAPTER TEN: PULLING BACK THE CURTAIN

"In reality . . .": Justice Peter Smith, Baigent & Leigh vs.
   Random House Group Ltd., Decision, April 6, 2006.

"I am not . . .": ibid.

"Ideas aren't protected . . .": Mark Rice-Oxley, "Did *Da Vinci
   Code* Break British Copyright Code?" *The Christian Science
   Monitor*, March 6, 2006.

"Cases involving copyright infringement . . .": Jon Griffin,
   "Copyright Alert After Court Case: Firms Urged to
   Safeguard Important Material." *Birmingham Evening Mail*
   (U.K.), February 28, 2006.

"This is how a writer . . .": Mark Rice-Oxley, "Did *Da Vinci
   Code* Break British Copyright Code?" *The Christian Science
   Monitor*, March 6, 2006.

"Blythe wrote notes . . .": Dan Brown, First Witness Statement,
   #108. Baigent & Leigh vs. Random House Group Ltd.,
   December 21, 2005.

"For every page . . .": Dan Brown, First Witness Statement,
   #157. Baigent & Leigh vs. Random House Group Limited,
   December 21, 2005.

"In the late stages . . .": Dan Brown, First Witness Statement,
   #154. Baigent & Leigh vs. Random House Group Ltd.,
   December 21, 2005.

"I add Blythe's research . . .": Dan Brown, First Witness
   Statement, #156. Baigent & Leigh vs. Random House
   Group Ltd., December 21, 2005.

"This is not an idea . . .": David Stringer, "*Da Vinci Code* Court
   Case Opens in London." Associated Press Online, February
   27, 2006.

"There's no mention . . .": Jill Lawless, "Writer Insists in British
   Court that *Da Vinci Code* Borrowed from His Work."
   Associated Press Worldstream, March 8, 2006.

"overawed by the . . .": Justice Peter Smith, Baigent & Leigh vs.
   Random House Group Ltd., #231. Decision, April 6, 2006.

"He was a thoroughly unreliable . . .": Justice Peter Smith, Baigent & Leigh vs. Random House Group Ltd., #232. Decision, April 6, 2006.

"That's why I write . . .": Maev Kennedy, "The Day Dan Brown Struggled to Follow the High Court Plot." *The Guardian* (U.K.), March 13, 2006.

"I couldn't possibly tell you . . .": Jill Lawless, "*Da Vinci Code* Author Dan Brown Takes Stand in Copyright Infringement Lawsuit." Associated Press Worldstream, March 13, 2006.

"It's as if you've asked . . .": Jennifer Quinn, "*Da Vinci Code* Suit Gets Down to Details." Associated Press Worldstream, March 14, 2006.

"New Hampshire is . . .": Sarah Lyall, "*Da Vinci Code* Author Offers Peek Inside." *International Herald Tribune*, March 14, 2006.

"Baigent and Leigh . . .": Steven Zeitchik, "*Code* Author Refutes Claim." *Daily Variety*, March 14, 2006.

"For them to suggest . . .": Sarah Lyall, "*Da Vinci Code* Author Offers Peek Inside." *International Herald Tribune*, March 14, 2006.

"I see no reason why . . .": Vanessa Allen, "The Weird World of Mrs. *Da Vinci Code*." *The Mirror* (U.K.), March 18, 2006.

"*Get this book* . . .": Justice Peter Smith, Baigent & Leigh vs. Random House Group Ltd., 199. Decision, April 6, 2006.

"In my childhood . . .": Dan Brown, First Witness Statement, #95. Baigent & Leigh vs. Random House Group Ltd., December 21, 2005.

"A star . . .": Kevin Sullivan, "Star Witness: *Da Vinci Code* Author Testifies About Doodles and Dates in Plagiarism Trial." *The Washington Post*, March 14, 2006.

"I am a novelist . . .": Jennifer Quinn, "*Da Vinci Code* Suit Gets Down to Details." Associated Press Worldstream, March 14, 2006.

"How *The Da Vinci Code* . . .": Justice Peter Smith, Baigent &

Leigh vs. Random House Group Ltd., #214, 215. Decision, April 6, 2006.

"With that in mind . . .": Justice Peter Smith, Baigent & Leigh vs. Random House Group Ltd., #216. Decision, April 6, 2006.

"Even if the central . . .": Hugh Davies, "They Took on the World's Highest-Paid Novelist, and Now They May Have to Sell Their Homes." *The Telegraph* (U.K.), April 8, 2006.

"This is not the case . . .": Mark Rice-Oxley, "Did *Da Vinci Code* Break British Copyright Code?" *The Christian Science Monitor*, March 6, 2006.

"It is a fact . . .": "Court Rejects *Da Vinci* Copy Claim." BBC News, April 7, 2006.

"By its very nature . . .": Hugh Davies, "They Took on the World's Highest-Paid Novelist, and Now They May Have to Sell Their Homes." *The Telegraph*, April 8, 2006.

"This is a good day . . .": ibid.

"As J. K. Rowling says . . .": NBC's *Today*. September 15, 2009.

"Part of it . . .": James Kaplan, "Life After *The Da Vinci Code*." *Parade*, September 13, 2009.

"Writing is a solitary existence . . .": ibid.

"that quietly smiling face . . .": New Hampshire Public Radio, "Writers on a New England Stage," May 19, 2012.

"I was a little daunted . . .": "Howard Gets His Way; *Da Vinci Code* Movie Special." *Mail on Sunday* (U.K.), April 20, 2006.

"The Catholic Church has nothing . . .": *The New Yorker*, May 23, 2006.

"Even as a visual aid . . .": *The Wall Street Journal*, June 22, 2006.

"mix facts into a fictional . . .": Bob Minzesheimer, "Nothing's Lost on Dan Brown as Long-awaited *Symbol* Arrives." *USA Today*, September 15, 2009.

CHAPTER ELEVEN: THE ISLE OF LANGDONIA

"That lawsuit really . . .": Francis Storrs, "The Dan Brown Code." *Boston Magazine*, September 2009.

"He used to be . . .": ibid.

"After devoting so much . . .": "Court Rejects *Da Vinci* Copy Claim." BBC News, April 7, 2006.

"I think the concern . . .": Kathleen Burge, "Closing the Book: *Da Vinci Code* Author Fences Off His N.H. House in a Quest for Security and Privacy." *The Boston Globe*, April 13, 2006.

"It sits right out there . . .": "*Da Vinci Code* Author Wants Home Fenced-in." Associated Press, April 7, 2006.

"It wasn't quite like . . .": Janice Kaplan, "For Dan Brown, Success Has an Unexpected Price." *Parade.com*, September 11, 2009.

"Probably my love of privacy . . .": New Hampshire Public Radio, "Writers on a New England Stage," May 19, 2012.

"She is the quiet power . . .": Vanessa Allen, "The Weird World of Mrs. *Da Vinci Code*." *The Mirror*, March 18, 2006.

"She is the major . . .": ibid.

"All my e-mails to Dan . . .": Zoe Brennan, "Did This Woman Really Write *The Da Vinci Code?*" *Daily Mail* (U.K.), January 3, 2006.

"Blythe is open . . .": ibid.

"[Blythe] was everything [Dan] wasn't . . .": Francis Storrs, "The Dan Brown Code." *Boston Magazine*, September 2009.

"She was like . . .": Zoe Brennan, "Did This Woman Really Write *The Da Vinci Code?*" *Daily Mail*, January 3, 2006.

"They are truly . . .": ibid.

"They say Bill Clinton . . .": Francis Storrs, "The Dan Brown Code." *Boston Magazine*, September 2009.

"On some level . . .": Bob Minzesheimer, "Nothing's Lost on Dan Brown as Long-awaited *Symbol* Arrives." *USA Today*, September 16, 2009.

"the kind of house . . .": ibid.

"I wish I *looked* . . .": NBC's *Today*. September 15, 2009.

"When I published . . .": Jennifer Quinn, "*Da Vinci Code* Suit Gets Down to Details." Associated Press Worldstream, March 14, 2006.

"I was a shy kid . . .": NBC's *Today*. September 15, 2009.

CHAPTER TWELVE: LIFE ON HIS TERMS

"I don't think . . .": Karen Valby, "The *Da Vinci* Sequel Has Landed." *Entertainment Weekly*, September 18, 2009.

"The whole industry . . .": Jeffrey A. Trachtenberg, "The Wait of the World's on Dan Brown." *The Wall Street Journal*, January 25, 2008.

"When a major author . . .": ibid.

"Those little quips . . .": Bob Minzesheimer, "Nothing's Lost on Dan Brown as Long-awaited *Symbol* Arrives." *USA Today*, September 16, 2009.

"I'm in no hurry . . .": "*Da Vinci* Author Ducks Controversy." CBSNews.com, April 24, 2006.

"I will not write . . .": Karen Valby, "The *Da Vinci* Sequel Has Landed." *Entertainment Weekly*, September 18, 2009.

"This novel has been . . .": Paul Revoir, "After a Six Year Wait, *The Da Vinci Code* Follow-up Is an Enigma from the Very Start." *Daily Mail*, April 21, 2009.

"When I was five . . .": New Hampshire Public Radio, "Writers on a New England Stage," May 19, 2012.

"I could barely . . .": O, *Oprah Magazine*, September 2003.

"There was a vast . . .": New Hampshire Public Radio, "Writers on a New England Stage," May 19, 2012.

"The thing that happened . . .": James Kaplan, *Parade*, "Life After *The Da Vinci Code*." September 13, 2009.

"The furor died down . . .": ibid.

"Common sense and justice . . .": "Authors Lose Appeal Over *Da Vinci Code* Plagiarism." *The Guardian*, March 28, 2007.

"The ban really put . . .": Nick Pisa, "How *Angels and Demons* Makers Sent In 'Fake Tourists' to Take 250,000 Covert

Images of Rome After Vatican Ban." *Daily Mail*, April 27, 2009.

"We didn't shoot . . .": ibid.

"For weeks we sent . . .": ibid.

"Like Langdon . . .": "Movie Q&A: Tom Hanks, *Angels & Demons*." *Daily Record* (Glasgow, Scotland), May 15, 2009.

"When I go to church . . .": Kate Whiting, "Why Tom's on Mission for Heavenly New Role." *Belfast Telegraph* (Belfast, Ireland), May 6, 2009.

"Both science and religion . . .": ibid.

"I'm not going to . . .": ibid.

"*Angels & Demons* is . . .": *The Christian Science Monitor*, May 15, 2009.

"The major players . . .": Michael Phillips, "Talking Pictures: *Angels & Demons*." *Chicago Tribune*, May 14, 2009.

"Their lodge was above . . .": Bob Minzesheimer, "Nothing's Lost on Dan Brown as Long-awaited *Symbol* Arrives." *USA Today*, September 16, 2009.

"In a world where men . . .": Letter to Scottish Rite Freemasonry, U.S.A., Southern Jurisdiction, October 6, 2009.

"[The Masons] are fascinating . . .": NBC's *Today*. September 15, 2009.

"beautiful blueprint for . . .": Hillel Italie, "Freemasons Await Dan Brown Novel, *The Lost Symbol*." Associated Press, September 15, 2009.

"Washington, D.C., has everything . . .": NBC's *Today*. September 15, 2009.

"You do not want . . .": Karen Valby, "The *Da Vinci* Sequel Has Landed." *Entertainment Weekly*, September 18, 2009.

"Reading *The Lost Symbol* . . .": Malcolm Jones, "Dan Brown's *The Lost Symbol*." *Newsweek*, September 15, 2009.

"Brown's narrative moves . . .": Nick Owchar, "*The Lost Symbol*." *Los Angeles Times*, September 14, 2009.

"Emotions are the one . . .": Maureen Dowd, "Capital Secrets." *The New York Times*, September 30, 2009.

"We are very pleased . . .": Pauline Askin, "Freemasons Hail Dan Brown's Latest Novel as 'Good Fun.'" Reuters, September 15, 2009.

"I've been through a lot . . .": NBC's *Today*. September 15, 2009.

"My faith is a work . . .": New Hampshire Public Radio, "Writers on a New England Stage," May 19, 2012.

"The irony is that . . .": James Kaplan, "Life After *The Da Vinci Code*." *Parade*, September 13, 2009.

"One of the great . . .": NBC's *Today*. September 15, 2009.

"I went in a hat . . .": Bob Minzesheimer, "Nothing's Lost on Dan Brown as Long-awaited *Symbol* Arrives." *USA Today*, September 16, 2009.

"Although I studied . . .": "New Dan Brown Novel *Inferno* Due Out May 14." Reuters, January 15, 2013.

"He is the same . . .": *The Boston Globe*, May 8, 2004.

"I wouldn't describe . . .": *The Boston Globe*, May 8, 2004.

"My writing process . . .": *The New York Times*, March 21, 2005.

"Blythe is a wonderfully grounding . . .": New Hampshire Writers' Project talk, May 18, 2004.

"The state is a cultural . . .": Riley Yates, "Granite State Novelists at Top of Their Craft." *Union Leader*, July 2, 2004.

"But when you . . .": Jeffrey A. Trachtenberg, "Booksellers See Savior in *Symbol*." *The Wall Street Journal*, September 15, 2009.

"I set out . . .": *The Front Porch*, New Hampshire Public Radio, April 23, 2003.

ACKNOWLEDGMENTS

AS USUAL, ETERNAL thanks to Agent Apex Scott Mendel, formerly known as Superagent. Followed by Peter Joseph at Thomas Dunne Books, an imprint of St. Martin's Press, as well as Tom Dunne, Sally Richardson, and Matthew Shear. A special shout-out to Margaret Sutherland Brown for possessing the unique talent to keep track of my whereabouts, a science that often confuses even me, and also to Joan Higgins.

Thanks to Paul Zollo, Jake Elwell, and Greg Mironchuk for all their help. Extra-special thanks must go to Ron Wallace of Creative Musicians Coalition for his eleventh-hour assistance that added insight and details that I couldn't have gotten anywhere else. The book would have been a mere shadow of itself without his invaluable help.

On to the buddies in various geographic corners who provide me with a place for me and my laptop to land every so often:

In New Hampshire, thanks to Cheryl Trotta, who helps me keep my life somewhat organized in exchange for massive amounts of brisket, chocolaty things, and decent Chianti, and Sam Trotta, to whom I will be forever known as Good Mommy, and a grudging admiration for the stubbornness of Cosmo, aka GETOUTTATHEKITCHEN; Dean Hollatz and Leslie Caputo, who I think at this point just shake their heads with pity at my luggage explosions and last-minute appearances for which I pay a required toll in the form of See's Toffee-ettes; and, of course, Bob and Reagan Poochie DiPrete.

In Charleston, thanks to John Willson and David Porter for making Monday nights so fortifying that I can then proceed to effortlessly slog my way through the rest of the week chained to the computer. Also to Michael Murray whenever he happens to land there.

Finally, thanks to Alex Ishii, for being good for something.